CREDIT
APPROVED

CREDIT APPROVED

KEVIN PILOT

ADAMS MEDIA CORPORATION
Holbrook, Massachusetts

Published by
Adams Media Corporation
260 Center Street, Holbrook, MA 02343

ISBN: 1-55850-111-8

Printed in the United States of America

D   E   F   G   H   I   J

This publication is designed to provide accurate and authoritative information with
regard to the subject matter covered. It is sold with the understanding that the publisher is not engaged in rendering legal, accounting, or other professional advice. If
legal advice or other expert assistance is required, the services of a competent professional person should be sought.
— From a *Declaration of Principles* jointly adopted by a Committee of the
American Bar Association and a Committee of Publishers and Associations

This book is available at quantity discounts for bulk purchases.
For information, call 1-800-872-5627
(in Massachusetts 617-767-8100).

Visit our home page at http://www.adamsmedia.com

To Lois,
my editor

TABLE OF CONTENTS

INTRODUCTION

Imagine the difficulty in planning a vacation if you can't rent a car or check into a hotel room. How does it feel to be unable to buy a house, even though you can afford the payments? Or to be passed over for a new job even though you are the most qualified. While the increased availability of credit has been a windfall for some, it has been financially devastating to others. Driven to imprudent spending by a society that worships status, many otherwise responsible people have found themselves overextended financially during the past decade.

It only takes a single event, such as a divorce, the loss of a job, or even a health problem to turn a budgeting problem into a financial catastrophe. Friendly reminders soon turn into less subtle demands and finally into threats. These financial problems are often resolved over time but the enigma of a negative credit report remains. As a result, people are often unfairly labeled by creditors as a bad risk and as a result often discriminated against.

Contrary to popular belief, there are those willing to give you a second chance. Often it is only a lack of knowledge that separates those who successfully re-establish their credit from others who don't. Even if you have bad credit, it is possible to obtain a major credit card, secure a car loan, or even to buy a house. And for those of you who have never even been given a first chance, this book can be a guide to establishing your credit and maintaining it. I hope the information within will be as helpful to you as it has been to others.

CHAPTER 1

THE EXPANDING ROLE OF CREDIT BUREAUS

Why is an entire town in Vermont having trouble borrowing money? Apparently TRW accidentally gave everyone in the town of Norwich, Vermont, a bad credit report. An anomaly, says TRW. The problem began with Margaret Herr, a Vermont housewife who works part-time for a Georgia company that gathers information for TRW on delinquent property taxes, among other things. In the course of her duties, Ms. Herr came to Norwich to acquire a list of delinquent taxpayers. Rather than looking up delinquencies, she simply obtained a list of taxpayer receipts and reported them to TRW. "No huge number," said a TRW spokesman when confronted by the *Wall Street Journal* with the error. "Probably less than 3,000 people." In a town with 3,100 residents. TRW refers to the Norwich predicament as "a very isolated incident," but the credit bureau files at all of the "Big Three" agencies are riddled with errors, inaccuracies, and outright lies. Although the deficiencies of the credit reporting industry have only recently been in the headlines, credit bureaus have been criticized almost from their inception.

Dun and Bradstreet pioneered the credit reporting business around the turn of the century by establishing a system to record how businesses repaid their debts. This information was obtained manually from individual creditors and was soon sold to parties interested in doing business with a particular company. Only records of debt repayment were contained in Dun and Bradstreet's reports, and they were available only to other businesses. However, the boom in home ownership in the 1940s and the discovery of automobile financing soon created a need for consumer credit bureaus, as Americans became more transient and more eager to borrow. Most credit bureaus were local agencies, and unfavorable credit could easily be erased simply by moving out of state— sometimes even to another county. Credit bureaus often kept records in paper files or in ledger books, which were updated manually. The steady advance of computer technology allowed bureaus to become increasing sophisticated and to create more complete files. Like J. Edgar Hoover, they soon found it profitable to glean as much information as possible on everyone it kept a file on. Soon more sophisticated computers allowed this information to be available nationwide, and the modern consumer credit reporting bureau was born. As the consumer credit reporting business grew more profitable, bigger bureaus swallowed smaller ones until soon five major bureaus, Equifax, Trans Union, Chilton, CBI, and TRW held a virtual monopoly on the credit reporting industry. Congress, troubled by the exponential growth of a totally unregulated industry with Orwellian tendencies, passed the Fair Credit Reporting Act along the way to protect consumers. Passed in 1970 when many credit bureaus kept files in manila folders, the industry soon found loopholes and vagaries in the law to continue unharassed toward the goal of a complete file on every living American. Before 1970, bureaus were not required to disclose the contents of a consumer's file to the person in question. When the Fair Credit Reporting Act ended this practice, bureaus simply added a fee—often ten times what they charged commercial customers. Required to investigate errors, they simply refused, or reconfirmed incorrect information. Limited by law to giving credit reports only to those "with a substantial business interest," they interpreted this to mean anyone willing to pay their fee. To this day, in spite of recent publicity, the bureaus and the credit providers, including banks and retail stores, continue to shirk their responsibility to credit consumers. While credit reporting bureaus claim an error ratio of only one half of one percent, recent consumer polls seem to show a much higher percentage of inaccuracies. A Consumer Union poll places the error rate as high as *49 percent* of all credit reports. Almost half of all credit files. An informal *Consumer's Report* magazine poll places the percentage of inaccurate reports at 48 percent. Yet credit bureaus continue to deny that there is a problem. "We have a vested interest in ensuring that our files are accurate," said John A. Ford of Equifax to the *Wall Street Journal.* "If our reports are unreliable as some say, credit grantors would be the first to complain." Or would they? Credit grantors, such as banks, mortgage companies, and other lenders, might well prefer having a lot of inaccuracies appear in a credit report to missing any correctly reported negative information. After all, one bad loan can erase the profits of several good loans. It is better, from the lender's standpoint, to deny credit to some who really do qualify than to have one "bad apple" slip through the process. "If your report has more bad stuff than the other guy's, I think I like that," says Ralph Spurgin, a top credit executive at the Limited clothing store chain, in a recent newspaper interview. According to this line of thinking, a credit report purchaser would rather deal with the credit bureau who can dig up the most dirt on its potential customer. The issue of cost has also caused foot-dragging within the credit industry, already engaged in a price war. More accurate reports would drastically raise the cost of consumer credit reports. No large credit bureau, retailer, or bank wants to see these costs rise, and so they continue to resist tighter controls on credit.

Even as credit bureaus grow sloppier, the demand for information is exploding. Employers use credit reports to screen potential employees. Landlords use the bureaus when renting. Insurance companies run checks before issuing life insurance. The demand for information has drawn the traditional credit bureau into areas far removed from credit relationships. Most credit reports, for example, will list, in addition to your credit accounts, where you work, what your business is, and often what your salary is. A more in-depth investigative report will include interviews with your neighbors, employer, and relatives regarding your "personal character." Although for most of us this information would not be damning, it is often gathered is such a haphazard way that errors are the rule rather than the exception. "Interviews" with neighbors are often nothing more than a couple of questions along the lines of "What kind of people are they?" According to a recent lawsuit filed against Equifax, these interviews often never even take place: negative information is simply fabricated to produce a juicier report. Muckraking analysts are often rewarded for digging up more dirt than the other bureau because of the increased value such reports have with the credit report users. The consumer credit report has become the *National Enquirer* of the personal information business. As credit bureaus seem to touch almost every area of our lives, the consumer credit bureaus' cavalier attitude is having increasing devastating consequences on the lives of many consumers. Take the example of James Russell Wiggins. After finding a good job as a cable television salesman, he was unexpectedly fired after his firm ran a credit check and discovered that the credit bureau had reported him as pleading guilty to a felony cocaine possession charge. After discovering his report had been confused with that of a James Ray Wiggins, Wiggins received an apology and a corrected credit report but never regained his job. According to current law, the credit bureau is in no way liable. Neither is the employer. Mr. Wiggins, as the consumer, bears the brunt of the credit bureau's sloppiness.

As technology improves, the traditional credit bureau is slowly evolving into an information warehouse. Already credit reporting agencies sell lists to marketers who profile individual households by income and spending habits. Pre-approved credit is regularly proffered to those who are deemed credit-worthy. But perhaps the most troubling trend of all in the credit information industry is the increasing integration of government information banks and the private credit reporting industry. Robert Smith, publisher of the *Privacy Journal*, gives several examples in a recent article in the *Business and Society Review*.

○ The Office of Budget and Management completed agreements that permit any federal bureau to obtain information within twenty-four hours from all major credit bureaus, information that can then be used by agencies like the IRS and in conjunction with federal loans, grants, or contracts.

○ The IRS is renting lists, most probably from credit bureaus, containing lifestyle information to cross-reference with tax returns in order to pinpoint potential tax evaders.

○ The Treasury department routinely monitors information in private credit card accounts to enforce restricted travel to countries such as Cuba.

○ Equifax is considering including state motor vehicle information in its portfolio of personal information.

Each subsequent advance in information technology seems to strike a blow against privacy.

Bowing to public pressure, the federal government is slowly beginning to take measures against credit bureaus. Six states have begun legal action against TRW, one of the largest of the credit bureaus. The state attorney general of New York, Robert Abrams, claims "TRW is masquerading as a mere library of credit histories when in fact it is secretly rating the credit worthiness of consumers." According to Reuters News Services, Abrams accuses TRW of issuing one difficult-to-read credit report to consumers and another simplified version to credit grantors. TRW is also accused, in the lawsuit filed, of offering a credit scoring system to subscribers that is not disclosed on consumer reports. Many members of Congress are less than pleased with the growing number of complaints against credit bureaus. Rep. Charles Schumer (D-N.Y.) recently called for legislation rewriting the Fair Credit Reporting Act because "the credit industry is out of control."

Hearings of the Consumer Affairs Subcommittee of the House Banking Committee spotlighted many consumers who had been devastated by credit bureau incompetence. Although most witnesses were victims of mistaken identity, in itself an innocent mistake, the arrogant and uncooperative attitude of credit bureaus in correcting mistakes clearly showed the need for new, more consumer-friendly credit reporting laws. Several measures being considered include free credit reports once a year (TRW has recently begun offering this service voluntarily in hopes of staving off legislation), automatic reports of new negative information, and substantial penalties against incorrectly reported information. The credit reporting industry and credit grantors are both lobbying vigorously against such measures, but the die appears to be cast. A good credit reporting bill will include the following:

○ A free credit report once a year.

○ Civil penalties for incorrect information (both the credit bureau and the reporting business to be liable).

○ Information to be disclosed only with written authorization.

○ Consumers to be notified whenever negative information is reported.

Take the time to write your congressman or senator. The credit lobby is strong, and only a massive outpouring of support will force a bill to be passed.

Although the credit reporting industry is under-regulated, and consumers do not have the rights they should in a free society like ours, credit bureaus are not invincible. As the oriental martial arts teach, an opponent's size and strength can often be used against him.

CHAPTER 2

HOW CREDIT REPORTING AGENCIES WORK

There are two kinds of credit reports; consumer credit reports and investigative consumer reports. Consumer credit reports list credit history, place of employment, social security number, and marital status. This is the most common kind of credit report and it is used primarily by potential creditors. The second kind of credit report, the investigative consumer report, provides much more detailed information. It is usually used by a potential employer or by an insurance company planning to issue a large policy. This kind of report contains detailed personal information such as general reputation and personal habits. Such information is obtained by interviewing previous employers, neighbors, or anyone else willing to share information with the bureau. Equifax is the largest supplier of these investigative reports, which are most often sold to the insurance industry. Although credit bureaus often claim that these reports are more complete and informative than a standard consumer credit report, too often very little in-depth research is actually done, and, according to some reports, "credit analysts" are often encouraged to make inferences and even tell outright lies. Characterizations such as "of questionable character" and "deviant behavior" apparently help to sell the service to companies who are more interested in digging up negative information than in knowing the truth. This kind of character assassination is often so blatant that the Federal Trade Commission has had to take action on many complaints against Equifax. Some examples:

O A Vietnam veteran erroneously reported as dishonorably discharged cannot get the bureau to correct the information.

O A Cleveland man, after several demands, receives a report containing gossip from his neighborhood.

○ The fact that a person filed a legitimate complaint with the Occupational Safety and Health Administration is contained in that person's Equifax report.

Equifax, which naturally denies any wrongdoing, continues to sell its investigative report. It also continues to claim that it performs an in-depth investigation. A friend of mine recently applied for a job in an insurance company that uses the Equifax service. The sum total of the investigation was a telephone call to his landlord to confirm where he lived and to ask "What kind of a person is he?" Equifax represented this as an in-depth investigation to his employer in presenting his credit report. Investigative reports can be obtained in the same fashion that regular credit reports can, and you would be wise to check yours at least once a year. Your character is a very important asset, and with the growing use of these reports in employment, you ought to keep abreast of what is being said about you. However, since this kind of report is seldom used in connection with obtaining credit, this book will deal primarily with the more-common consumer credit report.

THE "BIG THREE"

Three agencies virtually monopolize the credit reporting industry: TRW, Trans Union, and CBI/Equifax. Equifax's reach is not limited to the United States; it is also a primary credit information supplier in Canada. These three agencies probably account for more than 90 percent of the credit information market in the United States. The near monopoly they have on the credit reporting industry makes these companies extremely profitable. TRW Credit Data Services, a division of TRW, Inc. took in over $690 million in revenue in 1988 alone. The bulk of their profits did not come from consumers, who purchase their own credit reports, but rather "subscribers," or creditors who use their services and provide most of the credit data. Subscribers fulfill a duel role as both providers of information and users of credit information. For example, a large retail department store might report the status of each of its credit card accounts to TRW. When opening a new charge account, it might also obtain a credit report from TRW to insure that the applicant is creditworthy. Credit bureaus only report accounts that belong to subscribers. Subscribers may include banks, department stores, and finance companies, who probably both supply account information and use credit reports in opening new credit accounts.

One important thing to remember when dealing with any of these credit bureaus is that, contrary to popular belief, they do not share information with each other. If you think about it, that would be like Apple Computer telling IBM how they make their screen so clear. These are competitive companies, often fiercely so. They earn their profits by convincing consumer credit users, or "subscribers" that they can supply the best credit report in the industry. Often this doesn't mean the most accurate but rather the one containing the most dirt. As we mentioned in the previous chapter, subscribers such as banks, department stores and other lenders use credit reports to find negative information, not to look at the accounts you've paid as agreed. Each credit bureau's file on you is probably very different. There is also a good chance that one file will contain the most information on you. This file is usually with the most dominant credit bureau in your region. In the west, TRW dominates; in the South, East and Canada, Equifax; and in the Midwest, Trans Union. When the credit reporting industry was young, these companies all dominated as large regional firms and many of their customers have naturally remained loyal. Most local credit bureaus listed in the Yellow Pages will be affiliated with one or more of these national firms. Knowing which credit bureau is used by a potential lender can often help you choose where to apply.

WHERE DOES THE INFORMATION COME FROM?

In their quest to become more competitive, credit bureaus have become more resourceful in their methods of data collection. In some cases they may even cross the boundaries of legality. In general, however, they use several legal sources of information.

O   Current and previous creditors.

O   Public records.

O   Internal analysis.

O   Credit applications.

Current creditors are a bureau's best source of information. Most of these creditors are subscribers and have their computer records "dumped" automatically into the credit bureau's computers on a regular basis. Creditors provide information such as when the account was opened, what the highest balance has been, current address, social security number, and payment history. For example, if you have ever been late on your department store charge card, the department store's computer will record how many times the account was late and how late the payment was each time. Once a month, the department store computer will give this information to the credit bureau(s) computer. If you apply for a charge account at another department store, they will obtain a copy of your credit report from the bureau that they deal with and it will have the current status of your other account. The credit bureau charges the second department store for a copy of your credit report but the first department store does not receive anything for the information it provides the credit bureau. A former creditor's account may also appear on the credit report, even if the account is no longer in use. The computers of most department stores, finance companies and banks retain old account information and continue to report it to credit bureaus, often incorrectly showing the account to be open. The information may continue to appear on a credit report some time after the credit relationship has ended. This information would include any late payments or other problems with the account. Keep in mind that creditors seldom report payments that are less than thirty days late, so not every late payment will necessarily show on your credit report. If the lender is not a subscriber to a particular credit bureau, the account probably won't show up at all.

Many of these credit reports have a decidedly negative bent. For example, the only credit information American Express reported for many years were delinquencies. They did not report current accounts in good standing. Accounts that do not involve monthly payments are usually not reported to any of the credit bureaus unless they become delinquent. Even a doctor's bill or a utility bill can become a part of your credit record if it's turned over to a collection agency. Any time an inquiry is made in your credit report, a record is kept in your credit file. If, for example, you apply for a department store card and the store obtains a copy of your credit report, it becomes a part of your record for two years even if you fail to get the credit card. Having too many of these inquiries can hamper your ability to obtain future credit. Credit grantors often assume that someone with too many inquiries on his or her report is either trying to obtain too much credit too quickly or has been rejected by everyone else—even if the rest of their application is in good order.

Public records provide another source of information for the credit bureau's records. All court records, bankruptcies, and liens are scrutinized by credit bureau employees and reported. This includes any tax liens(even if they've been paid) or small claims court judgments, although if you are sued and there is no judgment against you, it will not appear on your credit file. Other legal filing such as articles of incorporation, DBA's (Doing Business As), divorce, or death may also appear in your credit file. Anything that is public (and a surprising amount of information is public) can find its way into a credit file.

Internal analysis is one of the fastest growing "value added" services credit bureaus are offering to their customers. Increasingly sophisticated computers are allowing credit reporting agencies to cross-reference larger amounts of data to look for inconstancies in your credit file. If, for example, one of your creditors reports your social security number as 124-12-3333 and all the others 124-12-3334, the credit bureau will often indicate a "file deviation," a warning sign that something is wrong with your credit file. Other cross-references could include aliases, maiden names, differing middle initials, spelling, or any other information contained on the computer. Bureaus have programmed their computers to be constantly on the lookout for those trying to slip through the cracks by using slightly different social security numbers or spellings in order to try to lose a negative credit file. Unfortunately, and contrary to credit industry propaganda, most file deviations are caused by creditor's files, which often contain misread or incorrectly inputted information. As a result, credit-worthy consumers are falsely labeled high-risk and even tainted with the implication of illegal activity.

The final and perhaps most often overlooked source of information is credit applications. Each time you apply for credit the information you provide feeds the credit bureau's "information machine." Any employment information, address information, or anything else you provide is added to your credit file. Applications are the source of most of the personal information you will see on your credit report. Employment status, marital information, residence history and other personal information can usually be traced to the seemingly innocent credit application.

To best illustrate how this process all comes together, here's a made-up example. A consumer, call him John B. Consumer, decides he wants to buy a car from Honest Abe's used car lot. The car he wants will cost $5,000. He has $1,000 for the down payment and wants to finance the rest. Abe in-puts John's name, address, social security number, former address, and employer and the same information for his spouse and gets a credit report on John. The credit report shows any bankruptcies, tax liens, or legal judgments against John as well as any accounts he may currently have or have previously had with any subscribers to that particular credit bureau. It will not show any accounts with creditors who are not subscribers. Items that might not show up include local charge accounts, private transactions, and medical bills that have not been turned over to a collection agency. The next time John applies for credit, his "file" will show an inquiry from Honest Abe's Used Cars. It may also contain all the updated information he supplied to Abe in his application (at least, the information Abe used to access the report), especially if he was granted credit. If Abe did choose to lend John the money and if he did report the loan to the credit bureau, any subsequent information updates would also appear in John's credit file. Any information John shared with Abe could appear on his credit file. Although credit bureaus obtain information from a variety of sources, there is information they cannot report in most cases:

O Bankruptcies over ten years old.

O Unsatisfied judgments over ten years old.

O Satisfied judgments over seven years old.

O Any other adverse information more than seven years old.

Excluded information can be obtained when used in conjunction with:

O Credit transactions over $50,000.

O Underwriting insurance over $100,000.

O Employment with a salary over $30,000.

O Renting or leasing a dwelling with rent exceeding $1,000 per month.

OTHER "CREDIT BUREAUS"

At one time a person was required to have at least two pieces of identification before cashing a check. Usually one piece of ID had to be a major credit card or check guarantee card. On the West Coast, larger stores seldom ask for a credit card, and some do not even require a driver's license. What happened? Many merchants now use sophisticated computer systems or outside services to guarantee the credit worthiness of customers cashing checks. Target stores, for example, use an in-store system that works based on your checking account number. If you have cashed a check in the store before and the computer recognizes the number, it will approve your check. Smaller merchants may hire an outside service to guarantee its customer's checks (for a small fee, of course). The merchant simply runs a driver's license number through a terminal, and the check guarantee service cross-references your driver's license number with its files to see if any bad checks have ever been processed through their system. This kind of service is probably not alarming to most consumers, who correctly balance their check books, but in the case of fraud or when a wallet and check book are stolen and used in a store by someone else (who really looks at the photo?), the consequences can be catastrophic. Since these checking information databanks do not consider themselves covered by the Fair Credit Reporting Act, there is little recourse for the consumer. Another database that many consumers are not aware of is that of CHEX systems. This is a database used by banks to access information about accounts a new applicant may have held at other banks. If a bank account has been closed or money is owed to a bank in relationship to a bank account, it is reported to CHEX systems. The information is left on the report for five years (compared to seven years on a credit report) and can be disputed in much the same way as a credit report, although it is unclear whether this reporting agency is covered under the Fair Credit Reporting Act.

Computers have created the consumer credit boom. What were once scattered bits of public information can now be consolidated into one computer and accessed at lightening speed, thanks to Texas Instruments and the Japanese computer chip industry. Information from computers is difficult for many of us to understand, and when credit bureaus intentionally make computer printouts difficult to decipher, the process of understanding your credit report becomes almost impossible. *Almost.*

CHAPTER 3

UNDERSTANDING YOUR CREDIT REPORT

Credit bureaus are information machines. They feed on data from any source that reports to them. This information is often in error and will not be corrected unless someone brings it to the attention of the credit bureau. The burden of proof, under current law, is on the consumer, not the bureau, and that is why it is important to review your credit report at least once a year. Unfortunately, credit reports are anything but easy to understand. The fact that each bureau uses a different format increases the difficulty of understanding exactly what is on your credit report. In appendix B, at the back of the book, are the addresses of the three major creditor bureaus. Order a copy of your credit report from each and use this chapter as a guide to deciphering each.

The three most commonly used credit bureaus are TRW, TransUnion, and Equifax/CBI. If you can read these bureaus' credit reports, you will be able to understand most other credit report formats, since most credit bureaus are either owned by or affiliated with one of these "Big Three."

TRW

TRW Inc. is the largest provider of consumer credit information services on the West Coast. After the acquisition of Chilton Corporation in 1989, TRW's market share grew even further. Yet in spite of the mammoth profits provided by TRW's information services (approximately $49 million in 1990 alone), this division accounts for only 11 percent of the gigantic TRW Inc's $343 million 1990 profit.

TRW's profile is perhaps the easiest to read of all bureau files. It begins with identifying information entered to obtain your credit report. This is the data supplied when applying for credit or requested a credit report: name, current and previous addresses, and social security number. Also included in the top section of the report are the date and time the credit report was run and your current address, employment, and year of birth. Below the introductory portion of the credit report are several columns that describe your actual credit history. You may wish to have a copy of your credit report in front of you. The columns are:

Account Profile This column gives an overall rating of a particular account. There are three ratings: Pos. for Positive, meaning an account that has been paid satisfactorily; Non. for Non-rated, which may include accounts that were thirty or sixty days late but are now current, settled accounts, and inquiries; and Neg. for Negative, which would designate collection accounts, charge-offs (whether paid or not), repossessions, and other more serious delinquencies. Either the letter A or the letter M will appear in one of these columns. The letter A indicates that the account has been entered automatically from computer files. The letter M designates a manual entry.

This column is probably the first one lenders will look at when reviewing your credit report. Naturally, if all accounts appear as positives, they probably won't look much further. The non-rated accounts will be scrutinized closely and, in most cases other than inquiries, considered negative factors.

Subscriber Name/Court Name This section actually contains four pieces of information: the creditor's or court's name, the status date, the date opened, and an abbreviated payment status of the account. The status date is when the subscriber or creditor last reported to the credit bureau. The abbreviated status can be one of several codes. The most common are:

Curr Acct — an account that is currently open and has been paid satisfactorily.

Curr was 30 — the account is now current but was thirty days late at some point (can also indicate 60, 90, 120, 150 or 180 days late.)

Curr was 30–2 — the account is now current but was late 30 days twice (can also indicate other periods).

Delinq 30 — currently delinquent 30 days. This can also designate 60, 90, 120, 150, or 180 days late.

Delinq 30 was 60 — currently delinquent 30 days was 60 days late.

Coll — Collection account. The account has been placed with a collection agency.

Charge-off — creditor charged off account as an uncollectible debt.

Pd Chg Off — a paid account that was a charge-off

These are the most common account descriptions.

Type and Terms There are several codes for the kind of account and the terms. The most common are:

CHG — Charge account
AUT — Auto loan
H/E — Home-Equity Loan
LEA — Lease
R/C — Conventional Real Estate Loan

The terms column will indicate the length of the loan or if it is revolving, REV.

Amount and Balance The amount column will list either the highest credit line the account had or the highest balance, whichever is the larger number. The balance column lists the actual amount currently owed.

Account/Docket Number This includes two pieces of information other than the actual account or court case numbers. The balance date gives the date the balance was actually recorded. The amount past due column indicates the amount that is overdue. It may also show when the last payment was made on the account. An example would be an entry such as LastPay 8-88.

Payment Profile This is a coded payment history of your account. "C" indicates that you were current for the particular month being reported, "–" means that the creditor did not report for that month, "N" indicates a current or zero balance reported, and a number from 1 to 6 shows a delinquency of one to six months during that month. The letter or number to the far left is the most current month. The letters or numbers to the right are the preceding months. For example, a payment history coded 321CCCCCC would show an account three months past due the current month, two months the previous, then one month, and current for six months before that.

Credit Profile report messages A variety of messages may appear on your TRW Credit Profile. The most common are:

>>CHECKPOINT> AKA Present on File. More Data May be Available Under AKA — There may be additional information available under another name.
>>>CHECKPOINT> ***NICKNAME SEARCH*** — Provides information under a nickname.

TRANSUNION

TransUnion is a smaller and much more private company than either TRW or Equifax, CBI. In fact, TransUnion's name does not even appear on its Chicago headquarters. The owner of TransUnion, Marmon Holdings, abhors publicity and would prefer that no one knew it was in the credit reporting business at all. In fact, you have to dig fairly deeply even to find TransUnion's parent company. Although TransUnion's actual earnings are not listed anywhere (they are consolidated with the parent company earnings), one can safely assume that they are profitable. The Pritzer family of Chicago, who own Marmon Holdings, are known for their astute investments and are one of the wealthiest families in America. Jay Pritzer, the family patriarch, is listed among *Forbes* magazines's billionaires. A man who has the resources to bail out a company as large as Pan American Airways (Pritzer recently offered such a bailout package) would not be involved in an unprofitable business.

As with the TRW credit profile, the TransUnion credit disclosure begins with basic information such as name, address, employer, social security number, etc. It also includes information such as previous employer, previous addresses, position, and income, if known. The rest of the report is divided into columns, much like TRW, but more difficult to read. The columns are mixed together but basically read as follows from left to right:

SUBSCRIBER NAME, SUBSCRIBER CODE, AND DATE OPENED

Account Number and Terms The codes for terms give the monthly scheduled payment or the number of payments. Some examples are:

M250 — monthly payments of $250, no term is given
36 x 250 — 36 payments of $250
36M — 36 payments, the amount is not reported

Collateral This lists any property used to secure the loan. A car loan on a 1990 Corolla would list that car as collateral, for example.

High Credit The highest balance you have had on the account.

Credit Limit The credit limit on the account, as assigned by the creditor.

Date Verified The last date this account was reported to the credit bureau.

Date Closed Date the account was closed.

Present Status The present status column contains several pieces of information. The first is the balance owing and the amount past due. These will be the amount showing as of the last date on which the information was verified. The maximum delinquency section of this column gives the date of the last delinquency as well as the amount and the MOP. The MOP is the Method of Payment. A code from 00 to 09 is assigned to the account to indicate if you have been late in the past. 00 means the account is too new to rate. 01 indicates a current account that has never been late. 02, 03,04, 05 are indications of 30, 60, 90, and 120 day late payments, respectively. 08 is a repossession and 09 a charge-off or bad debt.

Payment Pattern As with TRW, this gives a history of payment on the account. Instead of using a "C" to illustrate a current account, Trans Union uses a "P" to show a paid account during that month. If a number appears, it signifies the number of months the account was late during that period.

This column also includes a historical status of the account that gives the number of months the account has appeared in the credit file as well as the number of times the account was 30 days, 60 days, or 90+ days late.

Type of Account and MOP (Overall) Codes for various kinds of accounts such as "O" for open, "R" for revolving, or "I" for Installment accounts are followed by an overall MOP (Method of Payment). This is where TransUnion and TRW differ. TransUnion gives an overall rating on each account on a scale of 1–9, one being the best overall repayment history on that particular account. Lenders will often look at this column first, choosing to look in more detail at potentially negative accounts.

EQUIFAX

Equifax is the world's largest supplier of computer-based information. In addition to providing traditional consumer credit information it provides health information to the insurance industry and real estate and loan information, and is the largest credit agency in Canada. Earning $81 million in profit in 1989, it earned over twice what TRW earned in its information business. Unlike TRW, Equifax's only business is information. Equifax is the largest provider of investigative consumer reports, health reports, and, with the recent acquisition of Telecredit, check information. This is "Big Brother" incarnate and is by far the toughest agency to deal with. It often does not accept certified mail, for example, unlike the other large credit bureaus. One can only surmise that this is to allow more foot-dragging when investigating complaints (it's your word against theirs as to when your letter arrived). Many complaints have been leveled against both the company's investigative reporting division and its health division. Be warned that you may have even more trouble getting information from and having information corrected by Equifax than you will with other bureaus.

As with the other two bureaus, the Equifax report begins with basic information like name, address, date, social security number, and date of birth. Additional information like previous addresses and employment are listed at the end of the report. An investigative report, which is also issued by Equifax, will include more personal information, as well as several pages of "analysis" of your credit references. Personal information obtained from interviews of neighbors and other acquaintances will also appear. Such a report is sent to subscribers and will almost never be sent to a consumer. It is easy to read, unlike the consumer version, and much more detailed. The consumer version reads very much like those of other credit bureaus.

Name, Account Number, Whose Account This section contains specific information about the account, as well as who the primary holder is. If your spouse has an account, for example, and you have a card, it would appear on your credit report with an "S," for shared, in the "Whose account" column. Other codes are:

J — Joint
I — Individual
U — Undesignated
A — Authorized User, someone who has charge privileges on someone else's account but is not responsible for payment.
T — Terminated, no longer active, closed.

B — On behalf of another person, someone able to act on behalf of another, using a power of attorney or other instrument.

Date Opened, Months Reviewed, Date of Last Activity The date you initially established the account and the number of months it has been open. Check the "Date of Last Activity" on each account to be sure the information is accurate.

High Credit, Terms, Balance, Past Due and Status. "High Credit" is the highest credit line or balance you've ever had on the account. "Terms" is the amount you are or were supposed to pay every month. "Balance" is the amount currently owing. Check this column carefully for accuracy. "Past due" is the amount currently overdue, if any, and "status" is a current rating of the account. This is what creditors will look at first. The coding is as follows:

The first letter is the kind of account.

O — Open account 30 days to 90 days. This would include accounts such as American Express, which must be paid in 30 days, or other charge accounts at retail stores or businesses which do not receive payments but are paid in full in 30 to 90 days.

R — Revolving. An open-ended charge account that requires regular payments but can be used continually to borrow more or charge more, up to a specified credit limit. A bank card such as Visa or Mastercard is a good example of this.

I — Installment account. A fixed monthly payment and a fixed balance, such as an auto loan or a home loan, where you cannot access a line of credit.

Following the letter designation is a number designation very similar to TransUnion's.

0 — Too new to rate.

1 — Pays within 30 days, currently not late.

2 — Pays within 60 days, has been or is over 30 days late.

3 — Pays within 90 days, has been or is over 60 days late.

4 — pays within 120 days, has been or is over 90 days late.

5 — has been more than 120 days late.

6 — Has been late but is making regular payments under a debtor's plan or similar arrangement. This code is usually used when the debt has been restructured with the creditor or through Consumer Credit Counseling (more on this topic later in the book).

8 — Repossession; this will usually also include a note as to whether the repossession was voluntary or not.

9 — Bad debt; the debt has been charged off.

If an "R1" appeared on your credit report, that would indicate a revolving credit account in good standing. The rating in the "Status" column only indicates the current status of your account. The history of your account is usually listed right below the reference to the account.

Credit History and Disposition Once again the negative bias of the credit reporting agencies rears its ugly head. If your account has never been late, nothing is indicated. A potential creditor is not absolutely sure that an account is in good standing; the creditor reporting may simply be providing incomplete information. If you have been late, however, a large ">" appears under your account listing. This attention grabber is usually followed by a listing of the number of times you were late. This is reported by a listing of the number of days late followed by the number of times you were late in brackets. For example, 30(1) 60(2) 90(0) would indicate that the account was 30 days late once, 60 days late twice, and never ninety days late. Following this revelation is a date coding, which indicates when you were late and a status coding identical to the one listed in the "Status" column previously discussed. These codes might read as follows: 01/90-R5, 12/89-R3, 11/89-R2. This would list the account as being more than 120 days late in January of 1990, more than 60 days late in December of 1989, and more than 30 days late in November of 1989.

The last piece of information listed under each individual account is a report of disposition. Some of these may include:

Charged-Off Account — account is considered a bad debt.

Closed Account — account is no longer active. Report may indicate who closed the account, creditor or debtor.

Settlement Accepted — debtor paid less than full amount owing to settle the account.

Secured Account — indicates an account backed by a security deposit. Equifax is the only credit bureau to differentiate between secured accounts and regular credit accounts.

Collection Accounts, Court Records, and other information
Following your regular charge accounts, loans, and regular credit lines on the Equifax report will be collection activity. Once again preceded by the ominous ">," the date the collection is first reported is followed by the collection agency it is assigned to and the Equifax code for the original creditor. This code can only be understood by Equifax. Information on the last status is preceded by the amount owing. The account number and date of last activity is then listed. The information is fairly self-ex-

planatory, except that the address for the collection agency is not given. If you wish to take up the matter with the agency, either to dispute their claim or to arrange a settlement, you will have to contact Equifax for the agency's address and telephone number.

Court records are listed under a similar heading and contain information about any lawsuits that have been decided against you and liens that have been filed. The most common kind of lien is a tax lien. The record of the lien is once again preceded by ">" and the date the lien was filed is then listed. The court and case number are followed by the amount and the kind of lien. If a release is obtained, that information would follow, including the date the release was granted. If you have been sued but settled out of court or won the case, no record will be recorded. If you lost, a record will appear even if you paid the judgment. If you didn't pay, the credit report would indicate that you still hadn't settled the matter. Check court records very carefully. Mistakes are often made, and this can be used to your advantage.

Inquiries As with all other credit bureaus, Equifax lists credit inquiries last on its credit report. The list records the names of businesses that have requested your credit report. You will often see names you have never even heard of but there is little you can do but wait for the two-year retention period to pass. A written authorization is not needed to access a credit report, although that may change very soon.

READING BETWEEN THE LINES—YOUR CREDIT REPORT FROM A LENDER'S PERSPECTIVE.

Loans are generally made on the basis of what is called Underwriting Criteria. These are the basic rules to which a bank or lending institution must adhere when writing loans. One savings and loan, for example, has strict criteria for issuing auto loans. Applicants must have three past credit relationships with balances of over $2,500 that have existed for more than three years. If you do not meet these preexisting conditions, or underwriting criteria, you will probably be denied. They will not even consider your application, even if you have $100,000 in income and have been on the job for six years. Underwriting criteria are created not by a credit department but by an executive committee. Underwriters in a credit department cannot issue credit outside these criteria without jeopardizing their jobs, except under special conditions usually outlined in the credit criteria outline itself. If you do not meet the criteria, then unless you happen to know the president of the company or have a very large deposit, you will not get an auto loan at that particular savings and loan. If, on the other hand, you meet the criteria mentioned but also have some negative credit, the decision to issue you credit may be determined by an underwriter. If you have a plausible reason for the negative credit, you may be approved. Once again, it may depend on the restrictions placed on the underwriter regarding negative credit. If you have any negative items on your credit report, you should have a good explanation ready. The best explanations are divorce, sickness, or loss of job. The worst explanation is that you took on more debt than you should have (how does the creditor know you won't do it again?), or no explanation at all. So the best place to start in establishing or reestablishing credit is to call and get the potential lender underwriting criteria. You will need to talk to an underwriter. Most will let you know exactly what their criteria are. Some may not be willing to share this information with you, but it is worth asking. Another good strategy is to take a copy of your credit report to the lender and ask whether she would approve a loan for someone with a credit record like the one you are showing and with the information you have given on your application. Naturally the lender will be hesitant to give you a yes or a no, but tell her you won't hold her to it; you are just looking for an indication as to whether you should apply. Make sure you are speaking to someone with the power to make a decision. Although you won't get a definitive answer, you should be able to surmise whether it is worth the risk of another inquiry on your account to apply.

Lenders are not trusting people. This is especially true if you have any negative credit. They will scrutinize your credit report, assuming that you are trying to hide something. If, for example, you have too many recent credit inquiries, they may assume you are having difficulty getting credit because you are applying to so many places. Or they may think you are having financial problems and are borrowing as much as you can, which could increase your debt ratio. If you are over twenty-six and have no credit or very little credit, they may assume there is a reason no one will give you credit, even if you've never applied for credit before. Some other warning signs lenders may watch for are:

O Claiming high income but having very little credit or not owning a house.

O Claiming high income but having small collection accounts or unpaid charge-offs on file.

O Claiming to have credit but not having a credit file.

O Having too many open credit lines, even though they're not being used (potential for higher debt ratio).

Credit criteria are not all lenders look at when considering an application. They are, however, probably the most important. Lenders will often reject an application solely on the basis of a credit report. It is important to improve your credit rating as much as possible before applying for credit and then getting your story across to someone who can make a decision.

Understanding your credit report(s) is probably not the end of your quest. If you are like almost half of most consumers, you will probably find at least one error on your report, and possibly some negative information. Don't despair. The credit bureaus are not as invincible as many would assume. A consumer can fight these companies and win. There are more weapons at your disposal than you have previously imagined.

CHAPTER 4

IMPROVING YOUR CREDIT RATING

CORRECTING BLACK MARKS ON YOUR CREDIT FILE

Credit bureaus have a tremendous amount of power. What is contained in a credit report can limit your employment prospects, determine where you live, and even hamper your ability to travel. Although credit bureaus would have us believe that the credit system is infallible, it isn't. Credit bureaus are staffed by human beings, and humans make mistakes. Although credit bureaus claim that errors occur in only one half of one percent of all credit reports, according to many consumer advocates the error rate is really between 30 and 50 percent. Until 1970, credit bureaus were not required to do anything about errors appearing in credit reports. Up until that time consumers did not even have the right to see their credit report, let alone dispute anything on it. The Fair Credit Reporting Act, enacted in 1970, gave consumers some basic rights regarding their credit file. These rights include:

O The right to see your credit report for free if you've been denied credit in the last thirty days. If you haven't been denied credit, most credit bureaus will still send you a copy of your credit report but will charge a nominal fee.

O The right to dispute errors. The credit bureau must re-investigate any items you believe to be inaccurate.

O The right to file a consumer statement with your credit report explaining your side of the story.

These rights do not guarantee removal of errors from your credit file. If you dispute an error and the credit bureau believes your dispute to be "frivolous or irrelevant," it is not obligated to reinvestigate the matter. In practice, credit bureaus are reluctant to call a claim frivolous or irrelevant because their reasons for refusing to investigate must stand up in court in case the consumer should decide to take legal action. If the credit bureau requests that the creditor or "subscriber" correct the error, and the subscriber does not respond in a reasonable amount of time (usually thirty days, although by law up to ninety days), the item must be removed from the file. If the subscriber responds and confirms the item, even though it may be incorrect on the subscriber's own credit files, the item remains and the credit bureau's responsibility has ended.

As we will see in chapter 16, many "credit repair clinics" offer credit repair based on "little-known loopholes in the federal credit laws." The laws they refer to are primarily one law, the Fair Credit Reporting Act. Although some of the clinics' techniques do, in fact, work, they offer you nothing that you cannot do yourself. The Fair Credit Reporting Act is meant to be used to correct errors made in your credit report. Credit repair clinics often attempt to use it to correct legitimately negative items. Although this tactic can work, you would have to misrepresent yourself in order have these legitimate items removed, an undertaking that inevitably carries a certain amount of risk. If a credit bureau suspects that you are misrepresenting yourself or using a credit repair service, it may "tag" your account and refuse to act on future requests for re-investigation.

If you still owe money on accounts that are showing as negative credit items on your report, you would be well advised to skip over to Chapter 5 before attempting to implement any credit repair plan. Trying to improve your credit while you are still struggling with your debts is futile. Since most subscribers report almost every month, it would be of little use having negative items removed only to have them reappear in corrected form the following month. Wait until your overdue accounts are settled before implementing this program.

CREDIT REPAIR—A SIX-STEP PLAN

Step #1: Obtain your credit report and locate any errors.
Here are some of the most common errors.

O Accounts that are paid or closed showing as open or even delinquent.

O Accounts that do not belong to you.

O Accounts that are more than seven years old and thus should be removed (ten years for bankruptcies and unsatisfied judgments).

○ Accounts that are showing incorrect information, such as social security number, amount owing, etc.

You might think it unlikely that anyone else's account could appear on your credit file, but a new credit card scam that borrows your name and social security number was recently reported in the *Los Angeles Times*. It begins with an unscrupulous subscriber to a credit bureau. Since it is relatively easy for someone to obtain access to a major credit bureau's computer through a local credit bureau under the auspices of a legitimate business, all that is needed is a terminal and a modem. A person's name is entered into the system, calling up a list of people with the same name (the more common the name, the better). A credit file is pulled up on one of these people, selected for his or her good credit, and the social security number and other pertinent information are obtained. The information is then used to apply for new credit, which is usually never paid. These names and social security numbers are sometimes sold by unscrupulous credit repair clinics, which advertise in local newspapers. Credit bureaus do very little to stop this practice and often refuse to correct the negative information left on the victim's report, meaning that the person whose file was used is stuck with a black mark on his credit report that is almost impossible to remove. Indeed, credit bureaus do very little to limit access to their credit files. A *BusinessWeek* editor recently, with very little difficulty, obtained a credit bureau terminal and later a credit report on Dan Quayle and several other prominent politicians. The loose security measures provided by credit bureaus make it even more likely that an error may appear in your file. Interestingly, credit bureaus do not deny that these abuses happen. They have also been slow to limit access to their computer systems. More security means higher costs and smaller profits in an already extremely competitive environment. When asked about the Dan Quayle incident, one bureau spokesman responded that the inquiry was illegal and for that reason was not the credit bureau's responsibility.

Step #2: Notify the credit bureau reporting the error *in writing*.

Send a letter to the bureau letting them know which item is in error. Although you are not obligated to state why it is in error, it may help your case to explain. Certify the letter with a return receipt requested. If you do not hear from the bureau within three weeks, send a second letter, requesting, for a second time, that they investigate the error. Credit

Bureaus must respond to your request within a reasonable amount of time (usually defined as thirty days).

Three weeks after your second letter, if you have still not received a response and the item has not been cleared, write a letter of complaint to the Better Business Bureau, the state attorney general's office, and the federal trade commission. (Although only the BBB and the state attorney general's office will respond to individual complaints, the FTC does track patterns of abuse of the Fair Credit Reporting Act.) This will help to speed up the response. Some bureaus have recently implemented a nasty policy of not accepting certified mail. This insures that you will have no proof as to the arrival of or the time of arrival of your dispute or complaint. The glut of disputes and complaints they have been receiving has made many bureaus fall behind in their investigations. This problem can be rectified by complaining sooner, insuring that someone else has a record of your complaint. Since most of these organizations forward your complaint to the credit bureau, the bureau cannot say that they did not receive it. Appendix A lists the addresses of all Federal Trade Commission offices and state attorney general's offices. Look in your local telephone book for the address of the nearest Better Business Bureau.

Credit repair clinics often deluge the bureau with re-investigation letters on every negative item, valid or not. The hope is that the bureaucracies of both the bureau and the original creditor will cause the confirmation process to break down, making verification impossible. A creditor is less likely to respond to a verification request on an account that is fairly old, especially if it has already been paid. Older accounts and paid accounts are more likely to be removed if they are disputed. But creditors may get suspicious if they receive too many verification requests on the same account. Remember to dispute an account at one bureau at a time. You do not want to attract too much attention to your account.

When writing a letter of dispute, try to avoid sounding canned. A form letter may cause the credit bureau to deny your claim in the belief that you are working with a credit repair clinic. Make your letter sound as plausible as possible and put it in your own words.

> "This account is not mine. I've never had an account with this company. You must have mixed me up with someone else."

> "I've never heard of this company and I don't have an account with them. Please take it off of my credit report."

The simpler and more direct, the better. Say it your own way. The best reason for disputing a negative account is that the account is not yours. Since this happens a great deal and there has been so much criticism (not to mention lawsuits) directed toward credit bureaus regarding this kind of error, it is the most likely claim to accomplish your purpose. Other claims, such as "I've never been late" or "The address isn't mine" are easy to verify if in any way untrue. By disputing a claim, you want to place as much doubt as possible in the mind of the original creditor that you are the same person he has dealt with. Don't fill up the page with extraneous information: just give your current name and address, along with one previous address. The less information they have, and the more conflicting information they have, the less likely they will be to verify the account and decide against you, after which further attempts will be futile. Then too, the older the account, especially if it is paid off , the better the chance of the original creditor not responding. That is really the goal of disputing the account; having the creditor fail to respond and so force the removal of the account from your credit record.

Step #3: Contact the original creditor.

If the original creditor verifies the debt to the credit bureau, the bureau's legal responsibility to investigate has ended. The item may be reported in error, but the credit bureau is no longer liable. Trying to dispute the account again may prove to be successful, but sometimes a creditor will keep a record of your last dispute. Recent lawsuits have held the credit bureau responsible for a deeper investigation than a mere confirmation from the original creditor. In practice, however, this responsibility is difficult to force upon a credit bureau. Never write your dispute on the actual credit report, as many bureaus request. It will show the last time you disputed the same item and trigger an automatic denial of your dispute. Send the information in a separate letter. Reword it slightly. If the credit bureau refuses to reinvestigate (Equifax is the toughest to get more than one investigation from), write a letter to the original creditor explaining why the account is being reported in error. Once again, certify it and have a return receipt attached. If the creditor does not respond in three weeks, send out a second letter, again certified. If you do not receive a response after three weeks or if they refuse to correct the item, contact the Better Business Bureau, the state attorney general's office, and the Federal Trade Commission. This should, at least, force the creditor to respond. Make sure to attach any and all evidence that would help substantiate your claim. Sample letters are given in appendix B. Sending a copy of the letter to the president of the company and making a "cc." on the bottom of the original with the president's name often helps.

Step #4: Take legal action.

This is not as expensive or time-consuming as it sounds. Even if you cannot afford the time to go through with a court action, just being served and facing the prospect of having to send an expensive attorney and prepare a case is likely to make a creditor carefully consider the idea of correcting the alleged error. If you decide not to go through with the case, you can always drop it before the trial date. The more compelling your case, the more likely the creditor will be to comply with your demands. But beware of filing a frivolous suit! If you go to court without a good case, the judge could find you responsible for the other party's legal expenses. It is also unwise to file a lawsuit against a party you are still indebted to, unless you have a very compelling case. The creditor may attach a counter-suit for the amount owed him and make it difficult for you to drop your case.

Small-claims court is the most likely arena for such a dispute. You can represent yourself, instead of hiring a lawyer, and it costs only a few dollars to file and a few more dollars to have your former creditor served by mail. You can seek damages and an injunction to have certain negative information removed. In the state of California you can sue for court costs, loss of wages, attorney's fees, and, when applicable, pain and suffering in the case of negligent or accidental violation. If you can prove willful violation of the Fair Credit Reporting Act, which can be very difficult, you can also sue for punitive damages not less than $100 and not more than $5,000, in addition to injunctive relief. (To sue for more than the amount prescribed by state law, you would have to file in municipal court, which would probably require an attorney.) Once again, if you have a good case it is unlikely you would ever need to go to court. The creditor is likely to answer your dispute promptly rather than risk an embarrassing and expensive lawsuit. Since you can represent yourself and the creditor is likely to be forced to send a representative, you have a definite advantage in terms of cost. If the amount disputed is small and associated with an old account, the creditor may remove it to avoid the cost of going to court. Be sure that your creditor can be served in the proper venue. All businesses operating in a given state are required to have an agent of service and an office where they may be served. Call the company to obtain the address of their local office, if they are a national company, and make sure to have them served at that office. You can also obtain a name of the agent of service from your state's department of corporations.

You can also take legal action against your credit bureau if they fail to respond to your requests for an investigation.

Step #5: Go public.

If you can't sue because of venue, time, or geographical constraints, and you do have a legitimate, verifiable case, write your congressman. Send copies to your creditor, including the company president's office. Contact your local television consumer troubleshooter, your state assemblyman, the government agency that regulates your creditor, or your local newspapers. Be sure to send copies of all correspondence to both the credit department you are dealing with and the president of the company. It should at least elicit a response.

Step #6: Tell your side of the story.

If all else fails, file a consumer statement disputing the error with your credit bureau. Remember, the bureau is required to put the statement into your credit report for all to read. Be prepared to explain the situation *in advance* to any lender with whom you are applying for credit. If you are up-front and not trying to hide anything, they may very well accept your explanation. Stating that the credit bureau and creditor have been unwilling to assist you in correcting this matter may also spur action on somebody's part. An explanation along the following lines may get someone's attention.

> "This account has been paid in full. Both XYZ company and ABC credit bureau have failed to investigate this matter. The negative credit reference should not appear on my credit report."

Since most of those reading the credit report are customers of the credit bureau, the bureau probably won't want that statement appearing. Stand your ground if they refuse to put your statement in your report and inform them that you are aware of your rights.

If you are unable to correct all of your credit because you can't prove an error, don't despair: improving your credit file is only half of the equation in regaining your ability to obtain credit. If you can prove that you are now a good credit risk, you may convince potential lenders to overlook past mistakes.

CHAPTER 5

PROTECTING YOUR CREDIT FILE

PROTECTING YOUR CREDIT FILE

Do you ever wonder where all the junk mail in your mailbox comes from? What makes an advertiser so sure you'll be interested in lingerie or a new fishing rod? Are they just taking a stab in the dark?

Information has become the hottest commodity of the nineties. The tremendous increase in the data processing power of computers has led to the creation of "super databases," which contain vast amounts of personal information. Advances in programming have allowed the information industry to manipulate data for almost any purpose. For example, if a large department store is interested in attracting female customers aged twenty-five to forty with incomes of $40,000 or more who hold executive positions at large companies and have credit lines in excess of $10,000, it could easily purchase a list. You might think you could never appear on any kind of list, but your mailbox says otherwise. Even the most seemingly trivial action can put your name into a database and your personal information on the auction block to be sold to the highest bidder. Information can come from the most unlikely places.

THE USERS

In an age of lower profits and even lower budgets, retail marketers of all types have found it is no longer profitable to employ a "shotgun" approach to marketing. For many years marketers relied on massive mailings and media advertising to drum up business. This approach, though very expensive, was effective, since neither the airwaves nor the postal system was yet filled with clutter. As markets became more competitive, and postage and airtime more expensive, advertisers began to find their marketing campaigns growing simultaneously less effective and more expensive. Retailers discovered that in order to stretch their advertising dollars they would need to employ a strategy of "target marketing," advertising only to groups they perceived as having the greatest likelihood of using their product. First a marketer would do a survey of its existing clients to find out who bought the most and try to determine those people's common characteristics. Perhaps they all had middle incomes, or a certain kind of job, or resided in certain kinds of neighborhoods. Then the marketer would go about locating more people with the same characteristics in the hope of selling more of their product. They could begin by looking in their own credit customer databases, but this source would run dry very quickly, and besides, these people would already be customers. Where could they find more patrons?

THE LIST BROKERS

A good list broker can get a roster of people with practically any set of characteristics you could imagine. Rich people, poor people, blue collar, white collar, homeowner, business owner, and any other specification you wish to name. Many of the credit bureaus sell or supply list brokers with information. These lists can be based on credit reputation, income, type of job, or any other criteria the credit bureau may have. Information can also be obtained from a variety of other sources. For instance:

○ Information on the kind of car you drive and where you live is available at many state motor vehicle departments. A list can be purchased, for example, naming all the owners of Jaguars in a specific county. Computerized databases, quickly becoming available, mean instantaneous access, allowing someone to input a name or a street and obtain all the cars a person owns or all the cars in a particular neighborhood.

○ The Post Office's change of address form not only goes directly to credit bureaus but is also available to anyone who asks. The current residence of any P.O. Box holder is also available.

○ Compuserve, a computer database service, offers a service called Phone File, which contains the names, addresses, and telephone numbers of millions of Americans across the country. A name can be obtained simply by entering a telephone number; enter a person's name and state and a telephone number will be given.

○ The next time you use a discount coupon at a grocery store, your name and address could be going into a database. Many of the coupons sent through the mail are encoded with your personal information. When the coupon is redeemed through an electronic scanner at your supermarket, the information may be placed in a database.

○ If you make a purchase through the mail, subscribe to a magazine, or return a warranty card, the personal information you include is probably being sold to other marketers and information bureaus.

○ When you dial a toll-free 800 number, your name and address may be retrieved and the information you provide sold or added to a database.

○ When you check into a hotel and fill out a registration form, the information you provide is likely to be used again.

○ United States government agencies share information with most other agencies, including the IRS. Although most of this information is not available to private industry, government agencies do add to their files information obtained from private sources.

The list goes on. Although all of us enjoy the benefits of a computerized society, few realize the tremendous amount of information about our personal lives stored in private databases. Perhaps the most private and the most difficult to avoid having are the credit files and personal files held by the credit bureaus. These, next to government information banks, contain the most sensitive information about most of us.

THE CREDIT BUREAUS

The credit reporting industry is not only in the business of gathering credit information: it is also in the business of disseminating it. And not just to creditors and collection agencies. Bureaus sell their information to just about anyone. Case in point: as mentioned in chapter 4, *BusinessWeek*, a weekly business and financial publication, recently conducted an experiment. The editors wanted to find out how easy it was to obtain a personal credit report. They approached a small credit bureau affiliated with a large national bureau and told them they wanted to rent a terminal in order to run credit checks on potential employees. The bureau responded that for a monthly fee it would install a terminal in their office. No questions, no inquiries, not even an application. Using the newly installed terminal, a *BusinessWeek* editor obtained a credit report on Vice-President Dan Quayle that listed his credit lines, account numbers, and a great deal of other personal information. When confronted, the credit bureau responded that the action was illegal and that it shouldn't have happened. Imagine that the *BusinessWeek* editor was, instead, a conman who had decided you were to be his next victim. He could obtain your social security number and apply for credit cards under your name at a different address, or simply use the account numbers listed on your account and charge to his heart's content. Would the credit bureau's response then be, "Well, that was illegal and it's not our problem"? If others' past experience is any guide, it would probably take months, if not years, to have the incorrect information removed, during which the bureau would be of little or no assistance. Almost anyone can obtain a credit report. Most can even do it legally. All that is required is a "legitimate business need." Perhaps they are considering doing business with you. Perhaps they are considering offering you credit. It doesn't matter whether they ever do, they are only required to be considering you for a business relationship. This opens the door to just about anyone who is willing to pay for a report.

Credit bureaus not only furnish individual reports to just about anybody but also actively solicit business. Large credit bureaus produce some of the most accurate lists any marketer could want. Imagine a credit card marketer that is looking for customers for its Gold card. The only place it could possibly obtain a list of credit-worthy customers with certain current credit lines and income would be from a credit bureau. These lists are the source of unsolicited credit card offers, especially the pre-approved offers many of us receive in the mail. One need not be a credit card company to purchase these lists. I would imagine the only requirement would be a "legitimate business need," which could be just about anything. This credit bureau "moonlighting" is a source of tremendous profits, not to mention much of the junk mail floating around the United States Postal Service.

SIX STEPS TOWARD INSURING YOUR PRIVACY

Step #1: The first step in protecting your credit and name from unauthorized use is to get a copy of your credit report. You should do this every year or so. Look for unauthorized inquiries, accounts that don't belong to you, and other suspicious activity. If you spot anything out of the ordinary, contact your credit bureau and the creditors involved. If the report lists accounts that do not belong to you, you may also wish to contact the police regarding possible fraud.

Step #2: Contact the Social Security Administration to insure that no one is earning wages under your social security number. Call 800-234-5772 for a Request For Earnings and Benefit Estimate Statement. This will give you information about your social security earnings and benefits, which you can then check for discrepancies. The Social Security Administration allows you three years, three months, and fifteen days to dispute a mistake after it has been made.

Step #3: Contact your credit bureau and request that your name not be sold to outside marketers. This is a double-edged sword, in that erasing your name from these lists will mean you won't receive any more pre-approved credit cards. The value of privacy must be weighed against convenience. You can also opt out of most other private databases by contacting the Direct Marketing Association. Many of the members of this organization are list brokers and other direct mail marketers. They will remove your name from member organizations' lists, but you still may be on databases belonging to non-member organizations. The address is:

> Telephone Preference Service
> Mail Preference Service
> Direct Marketing Association
> 6 East 43rd Street
> New York, NY 10017-4646
> (212) 689-4977, ext.369

Many retail stores, banks, and other creditors also sell their lists to outside marketers. If you have credit cards, a mortgage, a checking account, or any other kind of bank account, your name, address, and telephone number may be used for other marketing activities, either by the company you are dealing with or by outside organizations. Contact these institutions and let them know you do not wish to have your information used for any purpose other than servicing the relationship you currently have with them.

Step #4: Obtain a copy of your medical information file. This file is used by insurance companies to rate your insurability. They may send the information only to your doctor, so include his or her name and address. The information contained in your medical information file is reported by physicians you may have seen in the past as well as your current doctor. Be sure the information is correct. The report can be obtained from:

MIB
P.O. Box 105, Essex Station
Boston, MA 02112
(617) 426-3660

Step #5: Check your motor vehicle records. This information may be available to employers. Ask how your state regulates access to these records. The obsessed fan who killed actress Rebecca Schaeffer in Los Angeles in 1989 obtained her home address from California's Department of Motor Vehicles. This prompted legislation allowing residents of that state to use addresses other than their home address in DMV records. Find out how your state regulates this information and consider giving an address other than your home, if permitted.

Step #6: Finally, don't give out personal information to anyone unless you know what it will be used for. Don't let merchants record your credit card number on your check. Use a post office box or other address when checking into a hotel. Don't give personal information such as address, social security number, or driver's license number to telephone solicitors. Beware of coupons and warranty cards. Once again, it may be wise to have a Post Office box or private box address to use on these kinds of responses. And get an unlisted phone number. It is worth the extra $30 to $50, because it will keep your name off many lists. Take reverse directories, for example, used by marketers to pinpoint specific areas where potential customers may live. A reverse directory is simply a telephone book sorted by street address instead of last name. If you want to look up telephone numbers on a certain street, you would turn to that street name for a list of the phone numbers, names, and addresses of everyone living on that street—everyone, that is, who is listed in the phone book. If you are not listed in the phone book, your name will not appear. The reverse directory is a favorite of stock brokers, insurance agents, and collection agencies.

Privacy is something that doesn't seem very important until it's taken away. In an age where everything is available at the push of a button, it is wise to manage the way the world sees you. Many of these databases, especially credit files, are the sum of your reputation. In today's tightening credit climate and in an increasing competitive job environment, your reputation could help augment your personal success or doom you to failure. Guard it carefully.

CHAPTER 6

ESTABLISHING CREDIT

The first time I ever applied for credit I was eighteen, just finishing my first year of college and trying to get a loan to pay my school bill. I planned on paying back the loan with the proceeds from a summer job I had just landed the week before. A bank is an intimidating place for someone whose only reason for entering in the past has been to withdraw money from a small savings account and to open a checking account the month before.

"Can I help you?" the new accounts girl asked.

"I need a loan," I responded.

She looked at me, sizing up my appearance and trying to ascertain my credit worthiness. "How old are you?"

"Eighteen."

"Do you have an account with us?"

"Yes."

"Do you have a job?"

"Yes."

She continued asking me questions, writing the information on an application form. I was then led to the loan officer who was to score my application.

"Do you have any credit?"

When I said no, the loan officer replied, "I'm sorry. I can't help you."

"Why?" I asked.

"Our bank does not lend to anyone without a credit history."

"Where do your customers get credit histories?" I inquired, not knowing any better.

"It's just our policy not to lend to anyone without a credit history."

Lenders do not like to lend to someone who has never borrowed before. The first credit relationship is by far the most difficult to get; difficult, but not impossible. I decided to take a tenacious stand.

"Let me speak to your manager."

I was led to the manager's office, a small, grey cubicle in the side of the building.

"I'm trying to get a loan to pay my school bill," I explained. " I will pay it back in three months. I have a job that will more than cover the payments. My father has dealt with your bank for forty years and all three of my brothers have accounts and mortgages with you. My grandfather opened one of the first accounts at this branch. Can I have a loan?"

The branch manager explained that the bank had a policy against lending to people without credit and then proceeded to explain how we could circumvent the policy. I got the loan for $1,200 and didn't need a co-signer. "No" does not always mean "no."

Don't be discouraged if you are having trouble establishing credit. Even if your family hasn't lived in a small town for seventy-five years, you can still establish credit with a bit of knowledge of how lenders work, and a little tenacity. There are really four steps to establishing credit;

O Establishing a banking relationship.

O Creating a solid credit profile.

O Obtaining secured credit or easy-to-qualify credit.

O Getting a bank card.

YOU AND YOUR BANKER

The banking industry has changed a great deal over the past twenty years. Once littered with small community banks, most areas now have only a few large regional banks and perhaps one or two smaller ones. Small banks that specialize in customer service and allow customers access to decision makers are slowly becoming a thing of the past. Bank managers have also changed from the days when they were able to make underwriting decisions on anything from a checking overdraft to a home loan. Credit decisions at most larger banks are now centralized. Only at smaller banks is there still some authority left at the branch level. If a bank has only one or two branches, you may even have an opportunity to speak with the president of the bank when applying for a loan. At the larger institutions, bank managers may have certain discretionary powers over such things as checking overdraft accounts, and they may carry some influence in the bank's centralized underwriting department. A recommendation from a bank manager will certainly not hinder a loan application. The process of establishing credit, then, begins by choosing a bank, or perhaps a few banks. Small banks often allow more interaction with higher-level employees, but large banks offer more consumer-oriented programs. They are also likely to report to credit bureaus, helping you establish your credit. Begin by opening a checking account. Try to get into your branch as often as possible. Talk to the employees and try to get to know them. A well-known customer is often perceived as a customer with more money. You would be surprised how many tellers will cash checks without identification from people they've seen around the bank several times. Find out who the manager is and who the loan officer is and try to get to know them. They can often help you to understand the underwriting criteria of the bank and may even help you to obtain credit.

The sharp dresser Have you ever noticed that a man in a suit gets better service than a guy in blue jeans? Merchants often judge a potential customer by his appearance. Driving up in a Jaguar makes a better impression on a new car salesman than puttering around in a VW Bug. A businessman gets a better table at an expensive restaurant than a construction worker. Many people judge you by your appearance, not least of all creditors. If you don't look credit-worthy, they probably won't extend you credit, so if you have the opportunity to meet someone who could have an impact on your loan application, such as a bank manager, try to look professional.

When filling out a credit application, think like an underwriter. How would the information you are putting down be viewed through pessimistic eyes? Emphasize your strong qualities and de-emphasize your weaker ones. If you're new on your job, make a note that you've been in the same profession for some time but happened to receive a better offer. If you've recently moved, don't forget to note that you lived at your previous address for some time. If you're a secretary, change your title to executive assistant. Don't be afraid of a little puffery. References are almost never checked, except for telephone numbers and possibly a confirmation that you are employed. The better you look, the more likely you are to walk away with a loan.

Secured loans Very often the only way a first-time borrower can get credit is through secured borrowing. In fact, the only exception to this is if you are in college or graduate school. Believe it or not, many credit card companies would rather extend credit to a student without a job than a stable, steadily employed worker. For some reason lenders consider college students extremely good risks. Credit card sign-up tables abound in campuses across the country. If you are a student, take advantage of these easy qualifiers while you are still in school; you may not be able to qualify after you graduate. If you are not a full-time student, you might wish to consider taking a class at a local Junior College. Many of these special college programs could then be available to you.

For those not academically inclined, a trip to your neighborhood bank may be a good start. Inquire into your bank's "savings secured" loan. This is a loan secured by a savings account or certificate of deposit. Ask whether loan information is reported to credit bureaus. If it is, consider depositing some money in the bank and borrowing against it. You may have to pay 2 to 4 percent above what you are earning on the account, but the account will be reported to a credit bureau, helping to establish your credit. Repay the loan and ask for a second, this time only 50 percent secured by the account. This is where a smaller bank will often have more latitude than a larger one. Continue this process, faithfully repaying each loan until you are finally able to borrow unsecured. If you can't find a bank willing to accommodate you, you may wish to consider a secured credit card, discussed in more detail in chapter 13. Checking overdrafts can also be easy to obtain. Sometimes they are even offered without a credit check (see chapter 12). But before taking out any secured loan, be sure it will be reported to a credit bureau. Otherwise, no one but your banker will know about your payment habits.

CHARGE!

Once you have established a few positive pieces of credit, you may be ready for a credit card. Contact the issuer first and ask to speak to an underwriter or credit analyst. Ask them what their underwriting criteria are. Many banks, especially savings and loans, offer credit cards only as a service and have stringent credit requirements. Don't waste your time and a credit inquiry on such places. Look for a consumer-oriented bank or savings and loan that doesn't view consumer credit as a necessary evil. Citibank, Chase-Manhattan, and Bank of America are examples of banks committed to consumer lending as a primary business. Their cards will probably be easier to obtain than those of a smaller, more specialized institution.

Department store cards are often even easier to obtain than bank cards and most are reported to credit bureaus. Gas company cards are also fairly easy to obtain but are usually not reported to credit bureaus. Another source of credit references often overlooked is mail-order catalogue companies. Many, like Swiss Colony, offer payment plans for purchases through their catalogue. Swiss Colony offers gift packages for the holidays. The company reports its credit accounts to all three of the major bureaus and does not run extensive credit checks on its customers. Other mail-order companies extend credit also.

A LITTLE HELP FROM YOUR FRIENDS

If all else fails and you can't obtain any credit on your own, consider asking someone to co-sign for you. A co-signer takes responsibility for your debt if you don't pay, so you probably won't want to ask a casual acquaintance for this kind of favor. The most common co-signers are parents and siblings, but a very, very good friend might agree to help you out. A co-signed account appears on the credit reports of both the primary signer and the co-signer, so you would want to make sure all the payments were made on time. A co-signer can be used on any kind of debt, from a credit card to a home mortgage. The person applying for the loan with you would be required to qualify in the same way you would.

Don't get discouraged if you are turned down the first time you try to get credit. Start small, with a secured loan, and work your way up to larger and larger balances and unsecured credit. Remember to follow these basic rules:

○ Make sure any loan you apply for will be reported to a credit bureau.

○ Find out whether you are likely to qualify before you apply. If you have too many inquiries on your credit report, you won't be able to get additional credit for two years, when the inquiries are removed.

○ Make sure you pay the companies that report to credit bureaus on time and you will soon be able to borrow for whatever you might need.

○ If you are turned down, write and ask the lender to reconsider. If you are turned down because of a lack of credit, list the credit relationships you have and any other personal factors (employment, length of residence, etc.) that might add credibility to your case. Be tenacious. Credit card companies are looking for a reason to give you a card. Afterall, credit cards are extremely profitable to the company: they borrow at 5 percent and lend at 19 percent or higher.

Once you've established your credit, treat it as a valuable asset.

Try not to pay late and don't go over your limit. If you have made mistakes in the past, don't despair. Contrary to popular belief, you can get a second (or third) chance.

RE-ESTABLISHING CREDIT

Most of the strategies given in this chapter can work equally well for someone recovering from a bout of debt. Although a bad credit report is usually much worse than no credit at all, most lenders are willing to listen to explanations. It is wise, however, to resolve your old debts before attempting to acquire new debts. A lender is not likely to understand why you would want to take on new obligations when your old ones have not been satisfied. Responsible debt management will help you obtain future credit, regardless of what your circumstances have been in the past.

CHAPTER 7

MANAGING YOUR DEBT

I've never met anyone with a credit problem who planned on not being able to pay her bills. Most people don't sit down and decide how to deceive a bank or a department store credit department. Rather, most credit problems result from one of two circumstances:

○ Unforeseen events. Divorce, the loss of a job, or unexpected medical bills are all very common reasons for negative credit. Most credit-granting institutions are willing to work with someone who is facing a catastrophic event, although even this is changing as bad loans rise and profits tumble.

○ A lack of planning. Sometimes people spend without thinking about how they are going to pay their bills. As their credit grows, the number of unsolicited cards multiply and their spending increases until they can no longer make their payments. By the time the realization of being in over their heads arrives, good credit is ruined and the borrower is unable to pay her debt, often forcing her into bankruptcy.

Prevention, rather than correction, is by far the best strategy for taking control of your credit. On the job, most people have a strategy for where they want to be at some future time; they have a plan and a time-table. Couples often have an idea of approximately when they wish to have children and when they would like to be able to buy a house. In the same way, everyone should have a credit plan detailing how much credit they want and to what purpose. A good credit plan should be only a means, not an end. Credit is a tool—not an ultimate goal, as some "consumer credit advocates" would have you believe. It is a means of achieving your broader goals, like financing a car, buying a house, investing in real estate, starting a business, or augmenting your lifestyle.

Gathering credit cards simply to be able to spend more is a path to financial destruction.

MAKING A PLAN

Credit planning begins with a budget. Creating a monthly budget not only helps you plan for your credit needs but can also help you track exactly how much you spend and where it is spent. Take out your checkbook and your latest credit card statements and add up how much you spent last month in the following areas:

> Mortgage payment or rent
> Groceries
> Household utilities
> Car payments
> Insurance
> Credit card/other debt payments
> Entertainment
> Household (minor expenses)
> Childcare
> Gifts
> Publications
> Club dues
> Medical/dental
> Clothing
> Miscellaneous
> Savings
> Charity

Add up the total that you spent last month in each category. Now take last month's paystubs and add up how much you made after taxes. Add in any other income you may receive on a fairly regular basis. Obviously, if your expenses (minus savings) exceed your income, you have a problem. You are either receiving more income than you are showing or using debt to finance your lifestyle. The latter course is a very dangerous one and will eventually catch up with you. In the column next to the one you just made, write in how much you think you should spend in each area. Add up the total; if it exceeds your income (minus savings, of course), go back and make cuts in discretionary areas. Some things cannot be cut, like mortgage, rent, or debt payments, so focus on the categories that provide you with the least personal "return on your investment." This will be your blueprint. You can now plan how to make use of credit. For example, if your clothing budget is $200 per month but there is a sale at your local department store you don't want to miss, you can finance your purchase on your credit card and deduct the monthly payment from that particular column of your budget. If you are in need of a new car, you can restructure your budget to provide for a higher monthly payment. Manage your credit as you would any other asset. It's very difficult to keep a budget, but it is essential in order to keep your credit lines under control. The worst way to use a credit card is on a whim. Never buy anything unless it is provided for in your budget, or unless you can rearrange your budget to pay off the item without adding any more expense than what you have already allotted. If you avoid "negative cash flow," that is, spending more than you make, you will probably never need to use some of the other chapters in this book. If you have already had problems with your credit because of overspending, now is the time to begin budgeting, to insure that you never have the same difficulties.

HOW MUCH IS TOO MUCH?

Credit is a double-edged sword. The more you have, the easier it is to get. If you have too much, however, even if you don't use it, creditors will not lend to you. So how much is too much? Well, obviously, if the total of your potential monthly payments exceeds the income you show, that's too much as far as creditors are concerned. Home lenders will usually limit your debt payments to 40 percent or less of what you make, and in today's economic environment this is a prudent maximum. When drawing up the payments column of your budget, calculate the maximum you would want to spend on credit card payments and stick to it. This doesn't mean you shouldn't have other lines of credit to use in case of emergency; just don't use those lines of credit. Resist the temptation to think of extra credit cards as "funny money." One woman went so far as to put one of her two charge cards into a safe deposit box so that she wouldn't be tempted to use it. She wanted it only in case of emergency. You may not need to go to that extreme, but try to keep credit cards "out of sight and out of mind." Get out of the habit of using credit for small purchases. Sit down and decide how you would pay your living expenses and bills if you were to lose your job and not find another for two or three months. In a case like that, if you hadn't saved a lot, you might need to finance your living expenses for a time. Make sure you have those lines of credit available.

SHOPPING FOR CREDIT—BEST BUYS AND WORST BUYS

Not all credit cards (or loans) are created equal. Many contain hidden fees. Some cards have low rates but no grace period. Many cards have a grace period but charge a much higher rate of interest. Many dealer-financed auto loans charge a higher rate of interest than what they advertise by using hidden fees. Lenders often take advantage of borrowers' lack of knowledge regarding credit matters.

When selecting a credit card, the first consideration is the condition of your credit history. If you have a bad credit history, you may be limited in the number of credit cards you can obtain. If you have a good credit history, or if you successfully re-build your credit history, you will probably be able to choose from a wider universe of credit card issuers. A credit card should match your lifestyle. For example, if you pay off your credit card balances every month, look for a credit card with a grace period and no annual fee. A "grace period" implies that the credit card issuer does not charge you any interest for a given period of time, usually twenty-five days. This means that if you pay when you receive your bill, you will not pay any interest on your purchase. The grace period is not necessarily twenty-five days; it depends on the cycle of your bills. The credit card company usually allows twenty-five days from the last date of your cycle, so if you buy something near the beginning of your billing cycle, you may not have to pay for a much longer time. For example, if your billing cycle is from the first of the month to the last day of the month and your bill is due on the twenty-fifth of the month, a purchase made on the first would not have to be paid for one month and twenty-five days. Look in appendix C for a complete listing of larger credit card issuers and their terms. Chapter 13 also goes into credit cards in greater depth.

Auto loans are another form of credit to be very wary of, especially dealer-financed loans. Often improperly disclosed, Rule of 78 loans charge interest up-front, making total payments much higher than those of a conventional auto loan. Although this is often the only kind of loan offered to someone with negative credit, it is much more expensive than a traditional loan. A 10 percent rate on a Rule of 78 loan, for example, could be equivalent to a 16 percent rate on a regular declining balance auto loan. Beware! Auto loans are discussed in more detail in Chapter 14.

The following are some of the best and worst buys in credit.

Best buys
O For those who carry credit balances, Wachovia Card Services. 11.40 percent Variable Interest Visa or Mastercard.

○ For those who pay their balances in full, USAA Federal Savings 13.70 pèrcent Variable Rate Visa or Mastercard. (For more complete information on credit card issuers, see appendix C.)

○ Discover Card. No fees; rebates; accepted by more and more merchants.

○ Department store cards. Usually no fees; liberal credit lines; often among the easiest to obtain.

○ Owner-financed mortgages. No points; low interest rates; but get a good real estate lawyer before signing (see chapter 15).

○ Auto loans with a down payment. 20 percent down gets you much more attractive terms than 100 percent financing. The interest savings can be substantial.

Worst buys

○ American Express. Why pay large annual fees for somewhat dubious status?

○ High-interest, high-fee Visa or Mastercards. Unless you have no other options, shop around.

○ Credit balance insurance. Why bother? Buy a term life policy from an agent and pocket the savings.

○ Rule of 78 auto financing.

This is just a partial list. Later chapters go into more depth on different kinds of credit.

The key to managing your debt is self-control. Resist the temptation to buy on a whim. Plan your credit purchases carefully and you'll probably never have to worry about not being able to pay your bills. Never get into the habit of paying for perishables with debt. Constantly charging dining and entertainment and then making monthly payments, or using one credit card to pay the payments on another, will definitely lead you to disaster. Using credit to finance such durable goods as cars, houses, and furniture while planning how to retire the debt is a far more prudent path. Spend a few hours a month planning your finances, including your credit. Set your financial goals and use all your resources to accomplish them.

Even if your financial situation is grave, it is still not too late to develop a strategy. Your strategy, however, may be slightly different.

CHAPTER 8

WHEN YOU CAN'T PAY YOUR BILLS

Minimizing the Damage

WHEN YOU CAN'T PAY

As the economy worsens, many credit-worthy individuals are having difficulty paying their bills. Perhaps they were laid off, or their employer went bankrupt. Payments slowly get mailed later and later, until one day the creditor who was recently anxious for business begins to harass the borrower: Pay up or else! Some creditors are more enlightened than others, but to most a person is simply a number, his or her worth based entirely on how quickly the bills get paid. Often there is only enough money to pay half, or a third, of the bills coming in. Everyone is calling and demanding money. Lawsuits are mentioned, and words like "deadbeat" enter almost every conversation. Who gets paid first?

KINDS OF DEBT

There are really three kinds of debt: secured, unsecured, and debts owed to the government. Secured debt is any debt with a tangible asset backing the specific loan taken out, for example, a home or car loan. If you decide not to make your car payments, the lender can take your car back and sell it to satisfy the loan. Secured lenders are likely to be the least flexible when you have trouble paying your bills. They don't really want to lose a good loan, but they know that they'll get a good portion of their money back by foreclosing or repossessing. This is especially true in a bad economy. When the price of real estate declines and the value of the loan exceeds the current value of the house, a lender is less likely to work out a payment arrangement. He wants to get the house and sell it as quickly as possible before the market drops even further. Paying back secured debt usually takes top priority.

Unsecured debt is extended by your signature only. A credit card, checking overdraft, or department store card are all examples of unsecured debt. In order to collect, a creditor would ultimately have to go to court, obtain a judgment, and then collect it by attaching your assets or garnishing your wages. This is a long and costly process. Even then, if you declare bankruptcy, you may not have to pay anything. Unsecured lenders are much more willing to negotiate on a late account, since they are much less likely to collect than a secured lender.

Government debts are almost always paid eventually. The most common debts owed to the government are federal or state income taxes. Neither the IRS nor the state income tax authorities are required to go to court, as other debtors are, before garnishing wages or attaching assets. Often only a notice that a bank account has been seized or that wages are being garnished is sent before action is taken. In spite of greater-than-normal powers, however, government agencies can be quite easy to negotiate with. They do accept payment plans from individuals and often take a few months before becoming nasty about collecting overdue taxes. State tax agencies are usually even easier to deal with than the IRS. If you are consistently delinquent, however, their docile attitude can change very quickly. Remember, with the IRS or the state tax agency, you have no rights. It is best to pay them as quickly as possible.

PRIORITIZING YOUR PAYMENTS

Once you've established that you cannot meet your obligations, you need to make a list of who needs to be paid first. Don't contact any of your creditors until you've established a pecking order. Bear in mind that you may have to change your priority list at a later date if creditors are unwilling to reschedule debt. On the top of the list should be your essentials:

○ *Shelter* (rent or mortgage payment). If you are in really dire straits, you may have to move your mortgage payment to the bottom. In most states, if a lender (say a bank) forecloses, the lender is not allowed to take any further action against you. The bank cannot foreclose and then sue you for any market losses it may have sustained in the property. If the real estate market has crashed and you owe quite a bit more than the house is worth, you may want to consider letting the property go back to the lender.

○ *Utilities and food.* Make a budget for both. Utilities can often be delayed as long as two months, but most companies are quick to cut off services after that. Contact your utility company for their policy on hardship cases.

○ *Transportation.* In most cities it can be difficult to get a job without a car. A purchased vehicle can be repossessed the day after your grace period expires, but most institutions will let sixty to ninety days pass before taking action. Even if repossessed, a purchased car can usually be recovered by bringing the loan up to date. Leased cars, on the other hand, may be harder to get back once repossessed, because the lender may not reinstate the loan. If you are late with a payment, contact your lender to see whether an extension can be negotiated. Always ask whether a restructured payment plan will have to be reported to your credit bureau.

○ *Bank or finance company credit cards and lines of credit.* Anything over thirty days late is reported to your credit bureau. Keep the cards with the highest available balance current first. You may need to use them in the future. Don't contact any of the banks unless you are sure you won't be able to make the payment. They can freeze a credit line or close it if they have any hint of potential default. If you must miss a payment, contact the lending company and ask whether it can reschedule the debt without reporting a missed payment to the credit bureau. Some larger credit card companies have provisions for these kinds of situations.

○ *Department store cards.* Department store cards, like bank cards, report anything over thirty days. They may also be more difficult to negotiate with because they may not have any special programs in place to help debtors restructure their debts.

○ *The IRS and state tax agencies.* Although these agencies have unparalleled rights in collecting taxes, they are also fairly generous in regard to payment arrangements, often allowing monthly payments. These debts will not affect your credit report unless a lien is filed. Be sure to ask when setting up a payment arrangement whether or not a lien will be filed. It usually take several months for action to begin. The IRS usually gets serious after three months and most states after about six months. If you owe money, try to make an arrangement before that time.

O *Gas company cards, and convenience cards.* Both of these generally require payment in full at the end of thirty days. This thirty days can usually be stretched to ninety days without losing your charge privileges. These debts are not reported to credit bureaus unless you are more than ninety days late. Many convenience card companies, including American Express, will also restructure your debt into monthly payments. You will lose your credit privileges, but nothing will show on your credit report. At the time this book is being written, American Express has begun to report all accounts, good and bad, to credit bureaus.

RESTRUCTURING YOUR DEBT

Most legitimate lenders do not want to take collection actions, especially in today's economic environment. If a lender has a debt that looks as if it may not get paid, the lender wants to get rid of it as quickly as possible, by restructuring it or making other payment arrangements or by having it paid off. When restructured, the obligation (debt) again becomes a "performing loan," a loan the lending company can include as an asset. If it is paid off, the company can take the money it set aside for a bad debt and use the money for other purposes. Even if the debt is only partially paid off, money is freed up from the bad debt reserves. This information can be used in two ways. The lender is likely to be inclined to set up a new payment schedule, restructure the loan, or settle the loan by full or partial payment and take it off the books completely. This is especially likely if the loan is unsecured. If the payments are long overdue and payment hasn't been made for some time, they may not trust you to make the payments you promise. On the other hand, if the obligation is not overly delinquent, the creditor may be more than willing to accommodate a new repayment schedule. Citibank, for example, has a credit renewal program for delinquent card holders that restructures the credit card debt by creating another loan with another division of the bank. It reports the former card account as paid satisfactorily and another account with the bank appears on the borrower's credit report. When negotiating with the creditor, make your circumstances sound dire but not unresolvable. Decide how much you can pay per month and offer it to the creditor in a restructured agreement. Insist that all old negative credit be removed.

If the creditor balks, suggest an agreement in which all negative credit will be removed after the debt is paid in full. Get it in writing: selective memory and high turnover could stymie your plan. If your account has been delinquent for a long time and you have only recently had the ability to pay, a creditor may hesitate before agreeing to a new payment arrangement. If the debt is quite old, be careful that you don't extend an already lapsed statute of limitation. If it has been longer than four years since the debt became delinquent, you may wish to approach the creditor by phone and have him send you a written agreement. If the creditor refuses your payment terms, offer a settlement. Settlements of much less than the amount owing are often accepted just to get the debt off of the books. Insist on having all negative credit removed. Start your offer at 40¢ on the dollar. Give the creditor some time to think about it; if appropriate, follow up with another offer. Everything is negotiable. Creditors operate like any other business people in that they are concerned with profits. You would be surprised how many will negotiate with you.

Consumer Credit Counseling Consumer Credit Counseling is offered in nearly every large city in the United States. It is funded by lenders with the specific purpose of helping borrowers set up manageable debt repayment plans. There are pros and cons to using this service. Since it is funded by retailers and other creditors, the advice often slants toward the creditor's best interest. Rarely if ever would they counsel the debtor to declare bankruptcy, even if that were the best solution to his woes. Most of the advice centers on budgeting and setting up a repayment plan by restructuring your debt. Though Consumer Credit Counseling can usually be relied on for decent (if jaded) advice, it does nothing for you that you can not usually do for yourself. If you are having trouble convincing creditors to reschedule debts, however, CCC may be a very good place to visit. Since they are funded by creditors and often deal with the same lenders, they may have the credibility you lack. It is probably best to use them only as a last resort, however, because debts that are restructured under a Consumer Credit Counseling plan are usually reported as such to the credit bureaus. Since they do have a close connection with lenders, they may also be unwilling to negotiate for removal of negative credit from your credit bureau files.

Incidentally, if you are simply unable to create your own budget and stick with it, you might consider visiting your local Consumer Credit Counseling office.

Preparing for the storm

Perhaps your Mastercard is only thirty days late. Sears has called to give you a friendly reminder. Your new job doesn't start for another month, and your wife hasn't found anything yet. There is still barely enough for rent, the car payment, and other necessities. Although you promise the person on the other end of the phone you'll be on time next month, you know the payment will be late, at best. It will be at least three or four months before you're caught up, and that's if everything goes according to plan. Don't wait for your creditors to take control of the situation. If you allow the payments to become too long overdue, you will get annoying calls, even risk being sued. When you are over this hump, the lender will be more likely to negotiate better terms if he feels the debt may be uncollectible. Get a private mailbox. Post office boxes can be used, but the post office is required to disclose the residence address of any post office box holder to anyone who inquires. Change all of your credit card addresses. If you do come to the point of a lawsuit, this will make it more difficult to serve you. Don't sign for any certified mail. If you are continually harassed by creditors, instruct them in writing (certified) not to contact you at work, and have your home telephone number changed to an unlisted number. It may be wise to rent a "voicemail box," which is a telephone number connected to an answering machine service. This number can be given to creditors to leave messages on and can be accessed from any telephone to pick up messages. The more difficult it is to contact you and the tougher it will be to serve you, the greater your negotiating leverage.

It is wise to take positive action as early as possible. It may appear that things will be better in a few months, but plan for the worst. Remember, there are tens of thousands of people who have been in similar situations and survived. Don't allow yourself to panic. There will be a lot of threats made. Debt collectors work on the principal of fear. Knowledge is your best weapon. The more you know about the collection process and the legal system, the less fear you will have when somebody calls.

CHAPTER 9

COLLECTION AGENCIES

How They Work and Why They Can't Be Trusted

COLLECTION AGENCIES

"No Recession in the Debt Collection" proclaims an article in a recent issue of an industry trade magazine. The article goes on to explain that collection agencies are making record profits as the recession causes more and more people to fall behind in their debts. Brokerage firms are recommending collection agency stocks as "hot" investments as we slip deeper into economic stagnation. Most collection agencies portray themselves as legitimate enterprises offering a needed service. Their business plan, however, differs greatly from that of a janitorial service or an accounting firm. Collection agencies are, very simply, in the business of creating fear. They prey on unknowing, financially distressed individuals. They are the scavengers of the business community.

Most people do not intentionally refuse to pay their bills. That would be stupid. Why not just declare bankruptcy? People do not pay bills because they can not afford to. A collection agency's goal is to scare, threaten, or cajole someone into paying its clients first. The collector doesn't care if you lose your car, can't pay your mortgage, or can't eat; they want your money so that they can make their money.

The only reason they even function is that consumers lack information. Not understanding their rights, or the restrictions put on a collection agencies, often allows people to be pressured into making decisions that are not in their own best interests. The first step in formulating a plan for dealing with collection agencies is to understand the collection process.

DEBT COLLECTION FROM A–Z

The debt collection process begins when you first miss a payment. A friendly reminder is usually sent letting you know that your payment is late. Mortgage and car payment reminders are often more demanding, since these debts are secured. If the payment isn't made, a series of letters usually follows, each increasing in severity. After anywhere from thirty days to six months, a creditor will usually turn the account over to collections. Many large companies, like Sears and Citibank, have their own collection departments. They save money by not having to pay a commission to an outside agency and are also able, in some instances, to skirt the Fair Debt Collections Act.

In-house collection agencies are not covered by the federal Fair Debt Collection Act, although many states have created state acts that apply to creditor-owned collection units.

Outside agencies derive their income from the commission they make on each payment they can force from a delinquent creditor. Commissions can range anywhere from 25 percent for a bill that will probably be relatively easy to collect to 50 percent or more on a very old debt. Collection agencies can also purchase debt from creditors at a deep discount and try to collect the money, keeping the difference between what they paid and what they can collect. While in-house collectors and those employed by an original creditor are usually paid a salary and a bonus, outside agencies generally pay their collectors on commission. Outside agencies tend to be far more aggressive. They can afford to be, since they have no relationship with the customer or any expectation of a future relationship other than possibly to collect more money. As in many sales professions, collectors are required to meet targets. They often tread on laws created to protect consumers and are not above using some fairly unsavory practices to reach their goals. According to a credit industry trade magazine, a collector's performance is usually rated by six criteria: the number of calls made, the contacts made, the promises made, the quality of the promises assessed by the percentage made, the percent of promises paid, and the dollars paid. Modern collection agencies use sophisticated computer programs to track the debtors and automatic dialing machines to harass them systematically. The bottom line is having money sent in so that the collector can receive a commission or a bonus. If the debt remains uncollectible, the collection agency will use progressively extreme tactics. In the end the matter may be turned over to the agency's attorney for legal action, provided a couple of criteria are met. First, the agency has to know where the debtor is and where he can be served; second, it has to be sure he has the ability to pay. The collector has a variety of methods for obtaining this information, which will be discussed later. If a lawsuit is feasible, the agency will usually ask for permission from the original creditor to proceed and then an action will be filed—usually in municipal court, since a collection agency is barred from suing in small-claims court. A frightening trend is the rise of law firms that double as collection agencies. For many years these firms avoided the Fair Credit Reporting Act requirements because they weren't considered collection agencies. To bring in business they often advertised that they could get away with things regular collection agencies couldn't. Fortunately, a revision to the Fair Credit Collection Act in July of 1986 imposed the same standards on legal firms as apply to any other collection agency. Legal firms often take advantage of their expertise and file immediately in municipal court. They may not even bother to check the facts of a case. They hope to take advantage of the consumer's ignorance and fear of the legal process, at times even going so far as to call the consumer and offer legal advice. Most consumers, having a certain respect for attorneys, succumb. This new breed of collector has a cavalier attitude about playing hardball. "We'll go after anyone, from a $40 bad check to a $40 million commercial loan," bragged one executive at a collection agency specializing in lawsuits. Don't take advice from anyone calling to collect a debt. Ask for the demand in writing. Refrain from giving any information other than a mailing address (preferably not your residence).

TRICKS OF THE TRADE

All collectors, whether in-house or outside, use a variety of interesting techniques. Some are perfectly legal, most are unethical, and too many are illegal but are practiced anyway.

The more information a collector can gather about you, the more likely he is to collect the debt or at least ascertain whether or not it is collectible. When he first contacts a debtor, he will try to get as much data as he can. First he will call you at work. If you no longer work with the employer listed on your original credit application, he will try your home number. Questions such as "Do you still live at . . ." and "Are you married" will usually precede the demand for payment. Listen carefully to the questions but don't answer any. Take note of what he asks you, because that is information he either does not have or is unsure of. Try not to confirm anything but simply insist on talking about the debt. After you've explained how dire your circumstances are, offer a payment plan, if you are able. The collector will almost always ask for more, usually an outrageously large amount. Tell him you can only afford what you've offered. He'll probably threaten you with legal action or worse.

Tell the collector that if he takes action, you will be forced into bankruptcy. If you can't pay, tell the agent you can't and that he should not contact you anymore. He will anyway, so be sure to write certified letters to the collection agency requesting no further contact over the telephone but only in writing at the address given. Any demands made or actions threatened should be in writing, something collectors are hesitant to do. If you continue to be harassed, write the original creditor, the state attorney general, the Fair Trade Commission, and the Collection Agency Regulatory Board in your state. If you are getting threatening phone calls, contact the police and the phone company and have a tap placed on your phone. Any more such calls will be prosecuted as an obscene phone call would be.

If a debtor can't be found, collectors have a variety of ways of locating him. The first clue to a debtor's disappearance is returned mail and/or a disconnected telephone number. A "skip trace" is initiated with a review of the original application. The employer who was listed will be called, as will the references, and the address listed may be physically inspected. The collector can use a reverse directory to get the telephone numbers of neighbors, who may be interviewed to try to find the skip's location. If these attempts are unsuccessful, a credit report will be run for additional information. Any other creditors on the list will be called to see whether they have any other current information. This last measure is an invasion of privacy on a tremendous scale. Many creditors will release personal information over the telephone to just about anyone who calls claiming to be a fellow bill collector. TRW and other credit bureaus facilitate this transfer by providing the names, addresses, and telephone numbers of all your creditors to any other subscriber who requests them. As has been noted, this can include just about anyone willing to pay the fee to set up a terminal. (One creditor I interviewed claimed that there is actually a "skip list" published somewhere—a list of the names of "deadbeats"—which is passed from firm to firm. As of the time of publication I've been unable to confirm the existence of this list, but if it is real, it is almost certainly in direct violation of the Fair Credit Reporting Act, which would require its disclosure to consumers.) Voter registration and motor vehicle records are also available to collection agencies and may list your most current address. It is very difficult, in the computer age, just to walk out on your debts. Unless you are able to relocate without letting your employer or any reference you have ever given or your neighbors know where you are going, you will eventually be found. It is a much better strategy to confront your problems, know the laws that protect you as a consumer, and conquer the fear you may have of confrontation. Of course, the harder it is for a collector to locate you, the better, so don't give information to anyone over the phone and do get a private drop box and an unlisted phone number, as discussed earlier. Have all motor vehicle statements and other traceable mail, as well as your forwarding address, go to the box. Don't give your residence address out to anyone. Instruct the owner of the mailbox outlet not to accept certified mail. Avoid coming to your box at the same time every day, and try to go there before or after business hours. This box, and a rented voicemail service, will allow collectors to contact you on your terms and will help eliminate harassment. Collectors will continue to harass you if they can find you, but there are methods to deal with them.

Harassment and your rights The Fair Credit Collection Act protects consumers from unreasonable collection action. Although the federal act only applies to outside collection agencies and to legal firms doing collection work, some states, as has been said, have passed state acts that have authority over in-house collection agencies. The acts prohibit the following practices:

○ Using profane or obscene language.

○ Threatening to harm you, publish your name, or get welfare or other government benefits discontinued.

○ Claiming to be a law enforcement official or to send your letters on what appears to be a court form or government document.

○ Contacting your employer, except to verify employment, or calling you at work if you request that they don't.

○ Threatening to take property or garnish wages, unless they have a legal judgment to do so.

○ Falsely claiming to be an attorney, or falsely claiming that legal action has begun, or falsely claiming the debt will be increased by fees.

○ Calling after 9pm or before 8am.

Many collection agencies could not care less about these laws. They will always insist on talking over the telephone, since it will come down to your word against theirs. Always respond to a collection agency in writing and certify the letter. If your rights have been violated, contact the state attorney general's office, the Federal Trade Commission, or your state's collection regulation agency, if there is one. Complain in writing to the collection agency. A debtor can also request that the agency cease all contact except for pending action, such as a lawsuit. If you don't want to talk to the collector or can't make an arrangement, you may wish to send him a letter telling him to cease contact (certified, of course). You should also contact the original creditor and let them know that you have been harassed. Bringing a small claims suit for violation of your rights is another action that can be taken. If the suit is valid, the collection agency will often settle by canceling the debt; you may even be able to receive monetary damages. Here are some examples of different harassment techniques used by outside collection agencies, both legal and illegal.

○ Claiming that if the bill is not paid immediately, wages will be attached the next day. Illegal. A judgment is required in court before wages can be attached, and you would have to be served before there could be a judgment. If there hasn't been a lawsuit, except in the case of income taxes, wages cannot be attached.

○ Threatening to tell employers about your delinquent bill. Illegal.

○ Threatening legal action when there is no intent to sue. This usually occurs on bills under $500. Illegal.

○ Repeatedly calling you for no apparent reason, just to rattle you. Illegal. One person retaliated by calling the collector three times for every one time he called him. He would ask stupid and redundant questions and use as much of the collector's time as he could. The collection agency's calls stopped.

○ Calling your neighbors, even though your phone number and address are known, and having them place a note on your door for them. This more subtle form of harassment is probably legal but very unethical.

○ Calling a former employer pretending to be an old friend and trying to get information. Legal. There have even been cases of co-workers being called and the debt being discussed.

○ Calling your family, especially parents, and discussing your debt with them. Illegal in community property states. In one case the family was continually called and the father asked for by name. The collection agent knew that he had passed away three months earlier but wanted to harass the debtor.

Note: These rules apply only to outside collection agencies in all states. Inside collection agencies are regulated under similar laws in many states, such as California.

The list of abuses goes on. Remember three things when dealing with a collection agency.

1. They cannot garnish your wages or take your property without a lawsuit (except in the case of automobiles, houses, and income taxes). You must be served and must have a trial before this can happen.

2. They cannot call you if you do not want them to. If a collection agency begins harassing you illegally, send the agency a certified letter requesting that it cease all contact. Inform the original creditor of the violations as well as the appropriate government agencies. If you wish to settle the debt or set up a payment arrangement, contact the creditor or the collection agency when you desire.

3. Collectors count on fear. That is their entire strategy. If you are not afraid and you understand the consequences that face you, their bargaining position is compromised. In the course of negotiating repayment, for example, if the collector threatens to sue, you can respond by saying that such an action would force you into bankruptcy and then nobody will be paid. Understanding what they can and cannot do gives you a great deal of leverage.

Trying to work out and pay off one's debts is not always possible. Creditors may be kept at bay for a short time, but eventually, if a satisfactory arrangement is not made, lawsuits and other actions against wages and property will follow. If there is no hope in sight, there may still be one option left.

CHAPTER 10

LAWSUITS, GARNISHMENTS, AND REPOSSESSION

How the System Really Works

LAWSUITS, GARNISHMENTS, AND REPOSSESSION

Anyone collecting a bill is trained to take advantage of two human emotions; guilt and fear. A good collector will usually start with guilt.

"You promised to pay and now you're breaking your promise."

"You lied when you made this agreement. What kind of person are you?"

If guilt fails to speed up your payments, fear is typically the next emotion to be manipulated. Bill collectors will commonly threaten a legal action, garnishment of wages, or repossession. Consumers, too often unaware of how the legal system works as applied to debts, are duped into straying from what may be carefully planned strategies. Collection agencies are especially notorious for these kinds of tactics, but large creditors are beginning to use them to a greater degree as they set up their own collection departments to save money and avoid the provisions of the Fair Debt Collection Act. There is one simple rule to remember when threatened with legal action: Don't panic. Your bank account cannot be attached, your wages cannot be garnished, and a judgment cannot be filed against you until you have been served. Collectors often try to leave the impression that they can take action without court sanction. This is simply not true in most cases. The only exceptions to the above rule are government tax agencies, motor vehicle lenders, and real estate trust deed holders. These three can take action such as garnishment or repossession without a court order.

If you fail to pay a large bill and refuse to contact the creditor to make arrangements, you are likely to be sued eventually. The creditor has only a limited time to take action (four years in most cases), so he is likely to sue as soon as possible if he believes he can collect. If you have debts you won't be able to pay for some time and you have ruled out the possibility of bankruptcy, you will still want to contact the creditor and make your situation sound as dire as possible. Be warned: he will try to gather as much information as possible, to be used against you later. Follow the steps detailed in Chapters 8 and 9: If he asks where you work, don't respond. Make use of a drop box as a mailing address and a voicemail as a telephone number. Don't give any additional personal information. Remember, the purpose is not to cheat anyone out of anything but to protect yourself. Although the Fair Credit Collection Act has been in place for several years, collectors generally ignore it, since most of their conversations are over the telephone and come down to your word against theirs. Never call a creditor or collector's 800 number from your personal phone if he does not already have your telephone number. These toll-free lines will indicate to the creditor the number you are calling from. The less information a creditor has about you and the more difficult you are to serve, the less likely he is to sue. Suing is expensive. If a creditor doesn't know where you live, or if you don't accept certified mail, he will have difficulty proceeding with legal action. He may eventually find you but by that time you may have exceeded the statute of limitations or be in a position to settle the debt. Before you go to these extremes, however, you should probably read Chapter 11 on bankruptcy. Bankruptcy is generally a better alternative than a life of dodging creditors. And often even the threat of bankruptcy is enough to turn the negotiations your way.

Any precautions you take may delay action for some time, but short of changing your address and job and not applying for any more credit, you will eventually find yourself facing a lawsuit. Legal action is probable when debts exceeding $1,000 are involved, but with the emergence of law firms that double as collection agencies, it is becoming more common on smaller debts. Legal action can take several forms.

LAWSUITS

The attorney will usually make contact before filing a lawsuit. A demand letter—a letter stating the claim and demanding payment—will ordinarily be sent a few weeks before action is filed. Sometimes it will explicitly state the intention to file a lawsuit. If it is ambiguous and uses words like "may take legal action," it may be a standard "dunning" notice. These kinds of notices are often sent out on an attorney's letterhead and are really mass mailings, not much more than another notice from the collection agency. A creditor may also call to inform the debtor that a lawsuit is being filed. According to the Fair Debt Collection Act, he may do so even if you have requested that he not call you. A final settlement may be offered even at this stage. If the creditor knows where you live and work, you may wish to work out an arrangement. Although you can probably make a settlement after a lawsuit has been filed, you will have more leverage at this time because the creditor would like to be able to avoid some of the costs of legal action. If the lawsuit is filed, the creditor may also insist that you pay legal expenses, which could be quite substantial.

There are three kinds of courts in which the lawsuit could be filed in: small-claims court, municipal court, or superior court.

Small-claims court Small-claims court is probably the most "user friendly" of the three. Attorneys are not allowed in small-claims court. Corporations must send an employee, officer, or director to represent them. Small-claims courts are generally very informal and are also limited in the size of the claim allowed. Limits vary from state to state, running anywhere from $1,500 to $5,000. The trend within the court system is to increase limits to relieve the growing burden of civil litigation from the municipal system. A claim begins with the plaintiff's statement. This is sent to the defendant (or the person being sued) by certified mail, the marshall's office, or a third-party agent. Different states may have slightly different rules on how a defendant must be served. A response is not required, but your presence on the date named is. In the case of a consumer obligation the *venue* of the case is very important. "Venue" is a legal term that refers to whether the case was filed properly. Although venue requirements may vary state to state, cases can generally be filed in the county (1) where the defendant currently lives, (2) where the contract was signed, (3) where the defendant lived when he or she signed the contract, or (4) where the goods or vehicle is permanently kept or installed. If the venue of the case is not correct, write the court and ask for a dismissal, stating your reasons why you believe the venue to be incorrect.

If the case against you is sound, you may wish to try and settle before going to court. If the creditor accepts a settlement, the case will be dropped and no judgment will appear on your credit record. Regardless of your circumstances, it is wise to appear on the trial date. If you don't appear, a default judgment will be given to the plaintiff, and although you'll have the right to appeal, the creditor will be able to take collection action against you based on the judgment. Even if you can't pay, it is best to appear, explain your circumstances, and, even if you lose, ask that the court impose a payment plan you can afford. If you believe you have a good case, present it to the judge when she asks for your response to the accusations. The questioning will usually go back and forth until everyone has said everything he wanted to, and then the judge will dismiss everyone and a judgment will be sent in the mail to both parties.

Large creditors tend to avoid small-claims court because they don't like to get company personnel involved in legal matters. The fact that a small-claims matter cannot be easily appealed is also a deterrent to most lenders. Since their size is an advantage, they will often use attorneys in municipal court. This may force the consumer to hire an attorney she probably cannot afford or go to court herself, which can be difficult at best. Since the rules of municipal or superior court are strictly defined (unlike small-claims court), an individual without legal training is at a distinct disadvantage. In the end it becomes a war of attrition, which large companies almost always win. Many large legal firms/collection agencies file large numbers of municipal suits using computers and paralegals, which brings down the costs of a suit dramatically. In spite of the difficulties, however, cases have been won by defendants without benefit of the advice of an attorney.

Municipal and superior court Any case can be heard in municipal court so long as the damages are less than $25,000. A $500 claim, for example, can be heard in small-claims court or municipal court. Creditors often choose municipal court for the reasons we discussed earlier. Any case involving more than $25,000 must be heard in superior court. A lawsuit in either municipal or superior court begins with a summons and a complaint. The summons indicates who is suing and where a response to the complaint can be directed to. The complaint can be several pages long and usually includes several statements of the allegations of what you did wrong. You are usually allowed thirty days to respond to these accusations. Although you can respond yourself to a complaint made in municipal or superior court, the process is not easy. If you have a good case and can afford it, get an attorney. If you know the allegations are true and you have no evidence with which to defend yourself, try to settle the matter. The creditor may agree to a payment plan but will probably insist on a judgment against you, although he is likely to dismiss the case if you settle in full before the trial date. He will probably settle for less than the full amount if you claim to have no assets or threaten bankruptcy. If you believe you have a good defense, you or your attorney will proceed as follows:

1. *Respond to the complaint.* The response usually affirms what is true in the plaintiff's complaint and then responds to what is not true, point by point. If a case questionnaire has been filled out by the plaintiff, you will have to fill one out also (it will be included in the material you receive). All this material is sent to the court or taken in by you and filed with the court. There will be a fee for filing your answer.

2. *Discovery.* Both the plaintiff and the defendant have the right to obtain information from each other. This can be done through depositions (sworn statements from anyone involved), requests for documents, interrogatories (questions to be answered under oath), and the producing of any other evidence that may be relevant to the case. If either side refuses to cooperate, the judge will order them to comply.

3. *Summary judgment.* Either side can ask the judge to make a decision based on the evidence at hand, namely the statements of the plaintiff and the defendant. This is usually requested by creditors' attorneys as a way of reducing their expenses. If the evidence overwhelmingly favors the plaintiff or the defendant, the judge may make a judgment. A motion called a "Notice of Motion and Motion for Summary Judgment" would first have to be sent, along with a declaration of the facts that support the judgment, all taken under oath. The other party is given an opportunity to respond to the motion. If the other party does not respond properly, the judge may very well rule for the other side.

4. *Pre-trial settlement.* A trial date will be set and you will be notified of a pre-trial settlement date. The creditor, you, and the judge will sit down and explore how the case can be settled. The judge, trying to prevent more crowding in the court's calender, will probably give you a fairly good idea of how she might rule, based on the evidence she has. If you have tried to negotiate a settlement but the creditor has refused to cooperate, be sure to make the court aware of it. Most judges hate nothing more than attorneys who waste court time. The judge may also be quite persuasive in convincing the parties to settle. This is your last chance before the trial, and if settlement is reached, there will be no judgment. Review your case carefully.

THE TRIAL

Not knowing the rules of evidence can be your downfall at the trial. There are very specific rules of what is admissible and what is not. Consulting your legal library will help. Organize your case so that it flows easily and each piece of evidence supports your assertions. If you have an attorney, you will be much better off in this phase of the lawsuit.

Defenses There are several good defenses for not paying a bill.

o The goods were never received or the service was never performed.

o The merchandise was faulty or defective or the service was substandard, both failing to meet contract requirements.

o The goods were damaged and the creditor was responsible.

o The statute of limitations has expired. Statutes of limitations vary from state to state. In California the statute of limitations is four years from the due date of the debt. On an installment debt, that means four years from the time each payment is due. So if you owed $1,200 to be paid back over twelve months and the contract was signed in January 1987 and you are sued June of 1991, then the statute of limitations defense applies only to $600, assuming you never made a payment. Although you won't destroy your defense simply by making a payment, if you make a repayment agreement, the statute of limitation begins all over again, starting on the date you make the new agreement. Never send a written promise into a creditor. Call and make a payment agreement and have the creditor send a confirmation of the agreement. Never respond in writing to a written confirmation. If you can't pay, the statute of limitations defense may be helpful to you at a later date. Check a local legal library for more information on your state's statute of limitations.

A lawsuit is not as bad as most people think. Even if you are sued, you have ample opportunity to settle before a judgment is made against you. Creditors often take advantage of a debtor's lack of knowledge and intentionally mislead him into believing that attorneys have greater powers than they do. A judgment has to be won before any other actions can occur, except in the three instances already mentioned. These need to be explored in greater detail.

SEIZURES NOT REQUIRING LEGAL ACTION

There are only three cases in which money or property can be seized without a court order: tax debt, motor vehicle debt (not including mobile homes and boats), and real estate debt.

Repossession A automobile lender can repossess your vehicle even if you are only a day late on the payments. The lender does not have to provide any notice; he can simply walk up and take the car. In practice, most give you more time than that to catch up, especially reputable banks and credit unions, but some finance companies and car dealers will be quick to repossess. This is especially true if they have information that you may not be able to make future payments, like a "friendly tip" from your future ex-wife or her new boyfriend. The creditor will usually hire a professional to retake the car, giving him your name, address, and any other information the creditor may have. They can take the car from any public place or from your driveway or garage, if it is open. They cannot break into your garage to retake your vehicle and they cannot confront you and physically force you from your vehicle. Once the vehicle has been taken, you have the right to reinstatement. If you make up whatever back payments you owe or pay off the debt in full, including any repossession, towing, storage, and legal fees, you can have the vehicle back. If your car is repossessed more than twice in one year, however, you may not have the right to be reinstated again. Reinstatement rights can also be lost if false information was given on the original credit application, if the vehicle is concealed in order to avoid repossession, or if the vehicle is not being properly maintained and its value is quickly depreciating.

The burden is on the creditor to prove that one of these conditions exists. Also, any personal property in the car must be returned to you. If the vehicle is not redeemed, a Notice of Intent to Sell is sent to the debtor within sixty days of the repossession. This gives you twenty days (depending on what state you live in) to redeem the car or pay the back payments, including any additional fees paid by the creditor. If your car is sold and the proceeds do not pay off the loan, you are also responsible for the excess money due, and you can be sued for it. The creditor usually sells the vehicle at fire sale prices, so a judgment for the difference, known as a "deficiency judgment" will occur in most repossessions.

Debts to the government The federal or state government can seize property without court action in the case of unpaid taxes. The action usually begins with a notice demanding the payment of your taxes, with penalties. The taxpayer filed and didn't include a payment, didn't file, or was audited and chose not to appeal. Several notices are sent out unless a person is labeled "Habitually Delinquent," in which case only one notice with a ten-day grace period will be sent, followed by immediate action. A notice to your employer of intent to garnish your wages will eventually be sent, and a levy against your bank accounts and other liquid accounts will follow, as will a lien, which will appear on your credit bureau files. The only exemptions from the liens and attachments are as follows:

O Wearing apparel and school books.

O Fuel, provisions, furniture, and personal effects.

O Business and professional books and tools of the trade, not to exceed $1,000 in value.

O Unemployment benefits.

O Undelivered mail.

O Certain annuity and pension benefits.

O As much income as is needed to make support payments to minor children.

O Minimum amount of income needed for sustenance.

The state can take a minimum of 25 percent of your salary and a maximum of 50 percent (with court approval). In practice, both the state and federal government have received so much bad publicity regarding collecting taxes that they are more than willing to work out payment arrangements. Many of these won't even affect your credit or require a lien to be filed. If the amount is large, however, and the payments you request small, a lien may be filed anyway. Call the IRS or your state tax collection agency early on to make arrangements. The tax agencies have access to most of your financial records, unlike private sector creditors, and are very good at collecting their money. It is much better to have a payment arrangement than to find your only bank account suddenly levied.

Foreclosure Foreclosure is a term that usually applies to real estate. Most real estate lending is done on a secured basis, so that if a homeowner fails to pay her mortgage, the lender has the right to seize the real estate she borrowed against. There are two kinds of foreclosure, depending on the state you live in: Trust deed foreclosure and mortgage foreclosure. A trust deed foreclosure requires no legal action. The lender merely files a Notice of Default with the county clerk. This does not mean a lender can file a Notice of Default and then walk into a house and take it over. Each state has a separate set of procedures that must be followed. Check with a local legal library for the foreclosure procedures in your state. Unlike a trust deed, a mortgage foreclosure usually requires court action. A lender must go to court and get legal sanction before beginning foreclosure. The only exceptions are in a few New England states where Entry Foreclosure is permitted. In this case the mortgagor evicts the owner and takes physical possession of the property, much as a landlord would evict a tenant. Legal action is not required. If you are facing the prospect of foreclosure, negotiate early. Even if the lender has issued a notice of default declaring the entire balance of the loan due, an agreement can often still be reached. Make your past situation sound temporary and present a plan as to how you will correct the default. The lending company does not really want to foreclose, but if it feels you won't be able to make payments at a later date, it will want to salvage as much of the loan as possible by foreclosing. Ask the lender to forgive interest, extent the term of the loan, or any other action that might help you to overcome the overdue balance. If the lender refuses to negotiate, look for refinancing. Unfortunately, if you're in default you may not be a prime candidate for a new loan. A new lender will likely charge quite a bit more both in points and interest. Using a good real estate attorney or constitutional attorney may buy some time to find a new lender. An attorney could also put pressure on the lender to negotiate by "throwing sand in the air." Don't pull any punches.

Even if you are in foreclosure and have no hope of redeeming your loan, you will probably have some time to adjust. It takes lenders anywhere from a few weeks to a couple of months, in most states, to actually have you physically removed. Negotiate with the lender for any equity you may have in the property. It could be traded for rent for a given period. Although there are a couple of excellent books on the market on foreclosure, there is no substitute for a good attorney in this situation. Such a person can help negotiate and perhaps save some of the equity you may have remaining. Avoiding foreclosure is usually why a mortgage payment should have a high priority in a budget, as discussed in Chapter 6.

THE JUDGMENT

Unlike the government, creditors may have difficulty collecting a judgment. They can attach 25 percent of your wages, but they have to know where you work. They can take your bank accounts, if they know where they are. Even when they've located your assets, there are some things that are considered exempt.

Although up to 25 percent of your wages can be garnished or taken, if you can prove that you need every cent to survive, you will be allowed to keep most of your salary. A Claim of Exemption will need to be filed by taking the "Earnings Withholding Form" that was given to your employer. The case will be heard before a judge, who will decide whether you should be exempt. This claim of exemption cannot be used for debts owed for necessities of life, such as rent, food, utilities, and medical bills. Certain other assets are also exempt, like a certain amount of equity in your vehicle and a certain amount of home equity. Some states even allow you to keep your entire residence and a certain amount of land if it is "homesteaded."

A creditor has the right to demand an "order of examination," which requires you to come to court and answer questions under oath concerning your personal assets. The creditor can only do this once every four months.

The biggest enemies a debtor confronts when facing legal action are fear and uncertainty. By understanding the process of a lawsuit, some of the uncertainty may perhaps be dissipated, and with it, some of the fear of facing a judge. Creditors, collections agencies, and attorneys don't expect you to understand the legal process. They will play on your fears and try to force you to make decisions that are not in your best interest. Know the process. The information in this book merely touches on the basics of civil legal procedure. Do some additional research if you face legal actions. There are always options. Don't trust the collection agency or the attorney calling you. He or she probably isn't giving you all of the facts and could be outright lying to you. Information is your greatest weapon.

CHAPTER 11

BANKRUPTCY: THE LAST RESORT

Negotiations with creditors have failed. Repossession is imminent and foreclosure proceedings have begun. Your income is simply not sufficient to pay your bills, no matter how low the payments are. It may be time to consider bankruptcy.

Bankruptcy law evolved as a reaction to the abuses surrounding debtors prison. Before the nineteenth century a prison system existed for those who didn't pay their bills. If a merchant filed a claim, the debtor was incarcerated until his debts were paid. (Women were not found in debtor's prison, not because of chivalry but because they did not have the ability to borrow). The lender was legally responsible for the expenses of the prison stay, including food, but seldom paid. After all, a debtor would have to sue in order to enforce this law, and it was rather difficult to sue when in prison. As a result, many borrowers languished in prison for years, surviving on what their family could bring to them or, in many cases, simply starving to death. Although some lenders would doubtless not object to the renewal of debtor's prison, fortunately we live in more enlightened times. Bankruptcy was created to provide a second chance (or third, or fourth) to those hopelessly in debt. It provides a mechanism to wipe the slate clean and begin anew. As times have changed, though, so has the bankruptcy code. Not all debts can be wiped out. The proceedings can be easily disqualified in the event of improper procedures. There are many things a debtor should know before resorting to bankruptcy.

THE BANKRUPTCY DECISION

There are two kinds of individual bankruptcy: Chapter 7 and Chapter 13. Chapter 7 bankruptcy, named for the chapter number in the bankruptcy code, requires a full liquidation of all debts and cancels all no-exempt debts. Chapter 13 bankruptcy is essentially a court-mandated payment plan that sets up affordable monthly payments to your creditors.

The decision to declare bankruptcy is not an easy one. Unfortunately, many bankruptcy attorneys recommend bankruptcy to just about anyone they consult with. All too often frightened consumers are advised to declare bankruptcy just to avoid a few debts. This is a mistake. Bankruptcy should truly be a last resort, as the legal system meant it to be. A bankruptcy appears on your credit for ten years, and although lending criteria are slowly changing, many lenders will not even consider an applicant who has had a bankruptcy. What's more, a Chapter 7 bankruptcy can cost you most of your property. Before making a decision to declare bankruptcy, estimate how bad your situation really is. On a piece of paper, make a list of all your assets and the approximate value they could be sold for. On the other side, add up all of your debts. If the debts exceed the assets by a large percentage, you may wish to consider bankruptcy. On the other hand, if it seems that your situation may improve (you may get a new job or a second income), or if your assets are of greater value or close in value to your debts, a different approach may be appropriate.

Negotiate with your creditors Explain your situation and ask for more time to pay. If the creditors refuse and continue to threaten garnishment, tell them such action would force you into bankruptcy. No creditor wants to hear the "B" word. Using bankruptcy as a threat is a very powerful negotiating tool, confronting creditors with a choice between getting a little each month or probably getting nothing through bankruptcy. Don't try this tactic on secured creditors. They may decide to repossess your property to avoid having to go through court.

Contact Consumer Credit Counseling As mentioned earlier in the book, Consumer Credit Counseling is a non-profit group funded by creditors to help consumers negotiate repayment plans. It is often able to negotiate payment arrangements better than the individual because of its constant contact with a variety of creditors. If you can't negotiate a satisfactory arrangement, give these people a try. Remember, the fact that you are using credit counseling may appear on your credit record.

Consider Chapter 13 bankruptcy This kind of filing allows you to repay your debts in a court-mandated fashion and will appear on your credit record for only seven years.

If negotiations fail or there simply isn't enough money to make ends meet, Chapter 7 bankruptcy may be your only option.

Bankruptcy does not necessarily discharge all debts. If your debts are exempt from bankruptcy, filing will do very little to improve your situation. If a co-signer was used, the debt would then be owed by the co-signer, unless that person also declared bankruptcy. In community property states a spouse's assets and debts would also be included in the bankruptcy, assuming they are community property. Consider all facts very carefully before deciding to file.

NON-DISCHARGABLE DEBTS—BILLS YOU HAVE TO PAY IN SPITE OF BANKRUPTCY

Certain kinds of debt cannot be automatically eliminated by bankruptcy filing. They must meet certain requirements before being eliminated by bankruptcy. If most of your debts are non-dischargable, bankruptcy may not solve your financial dilemma. The only ways a non-dischargeable debt can be eliminated through bankruptcy are through an exception being granted by the court, a certain period of time transpiring since the debt was due, or because the creditor does not object to the discharging of the debt. Certain debts can only be discharged by an exception. They are:

Recent student loans This applies to student loans that became due within the last five years. Any extension of repayment would be added to this time period. Some courts, furthermore, will only discharge payments that are more than five years past due. So if the student loan was due seven years ago and the payments were originally to be made over a five-year period, you would still be responsible for the last three years of payments. The court may also grant an exception to a student loan if it would produce an "undue hardship" for you to pay it. This is rarely granted.

Taxes Federal, state, and local taxes are not dischargeable for at least three years after you file your tax return. Even if you've been tied up in tax court for more than three years, any tax assessed within 240 days of filing for bankruptcy is non-dischargeable. Property taxes are dischargeable if they are over one year late, but the lien against your property is not. The bottom line is that you can count on the government collecting its tax money eventually.

Child support and alimony These can only be discharged in special circumstances, which generally include agreements that have not been court-ordered. If one spouse has agreed to assume more than half of marital debts in exchange for lower support payments, the court may not discharge all debts held by the spouse filing bankruptcy. Consult an attorney if this situation applies.

Fines Neither fines from a court, judge, or government agency nor surcharges, penalties, and restitution, as a general rule, can be discharged in a bankruptcy. The same is true of debts incurred as a result of damage or liability from driving while intoxicated. The debt incurred from intoxicated driving must be established in court and a judgment must be issued by a higher court. Small-claims, traffic, and municipal judgments for intoxicated driving are all dischargeable. Once again, consult an attorney.

Debts not discharged in a previous bankruptcy If debts from a previous bankruptcy have been found non-dischargeable, they cannot be discharged in a later bankruptcy.

Debts not listed on your bankruptcy petition If you do not include a debt on your petition, it will not be discharged. Many people filing bankruptcy keep one or more credit lines with small balances or no balance out of the bankruptcy proceeding to preserve part of their credit resources. Another strategy is to reaffirm debts on the condition that credit continues to be offered. The creditor, confronted with a choice between collecting nothing and maintaining your credit, will sometimes choose the latter. Be very careful when reaffirming debt. You are not obligated to and you should have a new written agreement spelling out all of the new conditions.

Other kinds of non-dischargeable debts can be discharged immediately if the creditor does not object. If the creditor objects, these debts will be judged by the court to be either dischargeable or non-dischargeable. The creditor can ask that the debts not be discharged if they claim the following conditions existed:

The debt was acquired by intentionally fraudulent behavior
Fraud in this case is any dishonest act used to obtain credit. Claiming to be someone you are not, or borrowing money when you have no means or intention of repaying it, would be clear-cut examples of fraud. Not disclosing certain relevant facts could also be construed as fraud. If you make a promise and intend to keep it and believe you will be able to keep it, that is not fraud. Creditors tend to be paranoid and believe eve-

ryone is defrauding them, so this excuse for non-discharge is often used by creditor's attorneys.

Debts incurred as a result of false written statements A blatantly false credit application would qualify. The inaccurate statement must be an important fact and one that the creditor relied on in order for the debt to be judged non-dischargeable. A misspelled name or minor error would not render a debt non-dischargeable. Drastically overstating income or misrepresenting a job title would be considered fraudulent.

Fraudulent usage If you charge "luxury goods or services" in an amount over $500 within 40 days before filing bankruptcy, the debt is likely to be deemed non-dischargeable. The same is true if cash advances are obtained fewer than twenty days before declaring bankruptcy. A lot of small charges, made to avoid pre-clearance, would also be considered fraudulent if you were over your credit limit or obviously unable to pay.

Debts resulting from illegal or malicious acts, embezzlement, larceny, or breach of fiduciary responsibility Any money owed because of illegal acts such as embezzlement (taking property left in your safekeeping), larceny (theft), or the failure to fulfill your duties as a trustee can be non-dischargeable. The court will usually determine a definition of fiduciary responsibility.

Once you've examined your debts and determined what is dischargeable and what is not, you can determine whether bankruptcy would enhance your current financial situation. There are several other things you should know before you decide whether to file.

EXEMPT ASSETS

A common misconception about bankruptcy is that you lose everything you own to satisfy your debts. In fact, the court will allow you to keep many things essential to your well being, and perhaps even a little bit more. Although there is a federal exemption law, only thirteen states and the District of Columbia allow you to use it. These states let you choose between the state and federal exemption laws. The thirteen states are:

Connecticut
Hawaii
Massachusetts

Michigan
Minnesota
New Jersey
New Mexico
Pennsylvania
Rhode Island
Texas
Washington
Wisconsin
Vermont

The other states require a person declaring bankruptcy to use state exemptions.

Here are some examples of things that may be exempt, depending on the state in which the petition is filed.

O Personal effects

O Furniture

O Cars (up to a certain amount of equity)

O Tools of a trade

O Equity in a residence (sometimes the entire residence)

O Clothes

O Household goods

O Books

O Jewelry

One very interesting exemption is the homestead exemption. When John Connally, the former governor of Texas, declared bankruptcy a few years ago, many people were surprised that he was allowed to keep his huge mansion, valued at several million dollars. Texas has a homestead exemption that allows anyone petitioning bankruptcy to keep up to one acre in an urban area or 100 acres in a rural area, *regardless of value*. The ex-governor may have had a very good attorney, but many other states also offer homestead exemptions.

One bankruptcy strategy is to sell non-exempt property before bankruptcy and convert it into exempt property. For example, a Texas resident might sell non-exempt assets and use the proceeds to pay off the home mortgage on her homesteaded property. You would almost certainly want to consult an attorney before attempting this kind of transfer of assets, however, since the court could very easily view such action as an abuse of the bankruptcy laws.

Even if a certain amount of equity is exempt, your creditors can often sell the asset to recover any excess equity you may have. If you own a car worth $10,000, for example, and you only owe $5,000 on it and your state exemption is $1,200, the creditor can sell the car and give you $1,200. Some states allow "wildcard" exemptions that can be used to cover the difference.

Knowing which debts are dischargeable and what the law allows a petitioner to keep, a rational decision can be made whether to file for bankruptcy. If you do choose to file, there are several ways of going about it—as well as several pitfalls to avoid.

TAKING ACTION

When you've decided to take action, you can begin the filing process. If creditors are knocking on the door and repossession, foreclosure, or garnishment is just around the corner, it may be wise to consider using an emergency filing to obtain an automatic stay. An automatic stay stops creditors from taking any further action until the case goes before a bankruptcy judge. Unlike a bankruptcy filing, which usually contains several pages of information, an emergency filing is only one page long and contains a list of your creditors. The rest of the petition has to be filed within fourteen days or the case is dropped. The court will send notices of the pending bankruptcy to the creditors listed, who must cease all further collection action. If they do not cease, send them copies of the automatic stay and request that all further collection action cease. A creditor can ask that the automatic stay be lifted, allowing him to continue collection action. Only a landlord trying to evict you from a rented dwelling will usually prevail, unless there is a long-term lease involved. If you are renting on a long-term lease, which could be considered an asset, the landlord may have to wait for a formal filing in order to evict you.

Once the wolves are at bay, another decision will need to be made: whether to hire a bankruptcy attorney. Attorneys, as we all know, are expensive. In the case of a complicated bankruptcy, however, they can be invaluable. If you have quite a bit of property or valuables, if you are trying to move money from non-exempt to exempt assets, if your creditors try to make your debts non-dischargeable because of fraud, or if there are any other complications, you may wish to hire an experienced bankruptcy attorney. Shop around. Don't be afraid to negotiate. Ask a lot of questions and talk to several attorneys before you make your decision.

If you have a very simple bankruptcy or can't afford an attorney, invest $15 in a good do-it-yourself bankruptcy book. It will give in-depth information not covered in this chapter. Typing services are also available to type up bankruptcy forms. They are reasonably priced and, in the case of a very simple bankruptcy, can take the place of an attorney. If your case is complicated and you can't afford an attorney, do your own research. Read a consumer bankruptcy manual first and then consult a good legal library. There are several legal guides devoted strictly to bankruptcy. Once you or your attorney have prepared your case, you're ready for formal filing.

THE FILING PROCESS

All the appropriate papers can be obtained from your local bankruptcy court. Consult the yellow pages under Government Services (usually in the beginning of the book) for an address and phone number. The court allows you fourteen days from the date of an emergency filing to complete the formal process. If Chapter 7 bankruptcy is being filed, you will need to send in the following forms after you have received them from the court:

○ Statement of Financial Affairs.

○ Schedule of Current Income and Current Expenditures.

○ A schedule describing your debts.

○ A schedule describing your property.

○ A schedule listing exempt property.

○ A summary of the above schedules.

○ Statement of Intention in regard to your secured property and what you intend to do with it.

○ Statement of Executory Contracts describing contract that will need to be fulfilled, such as auto leases.

○ Bankruptcy Petition cover sheet.

○ Mailing addresses of all creditors.

○ Any required local forms.

A fee will also be assessed, usually $90, due at the time of filing. The court will usually accept installments of a four-month period. An application for installments must accompany the petition.

After your petition is filed, a meeting of the creditors will be arranged. The court appoints a trustee to preside over the meeting and to be responsible for the liquidation of assets. With most smaller bankruptcies, only the person filing and the trustee will attend. The trustee, who is usually a local attorney, will ask several questions about the information on the bankruptcy documents. Call and ask the court clerk what papers you will need to bring (usually financial statements or sometimes even tax returns). If a lot of property is involved, especially if it is nonexempt property, your creditors may show up to protest any exemptions. They may also attempt to grill you about your intent to pay the bill or about lying on your application. Answer truthfully and there shouldn't be a problem. If the creditors' attorneys become abusive, demand a hearing before the bankruptcy judge before the proceeding goes any further. If the creditors object to any of your exemptions, they have thirty days after the creditor's meeting to file an objection with the court. The court will schedule a hearing and you will be given the opportunity to respond, although you don't have to. A creditor may also try to claim a debt as non-dischargeable because of fraudulent acts, a willful or malicious act, or embezzlement or theft. He can only accomplish this if he successfully raises the objection within sixty days of the creditors' meeting. To defend yourself, you or your attorney will have to file a written response and be prepared to argue your case in court.

Once all the requirements have been met and your intentions have been made clear, the court can declare the bankruptcy discharged. No formal hearing will be held unless you have chosen to reaffirm your debt, in which case the judge will want to be sure that you understand what you are doing. After this time, provided the creditors do not raise any objections, the dischargeable debts are erased.

PICKING UP THE PIECES

Bankruptcy was once the lowest disgrace that could befall someone. Today, however, it is commonplace. Corporations declare bankruptcy to get out of contracts or avoid legal judgments. Individuals rely on it to protect them from a society that extends credit too quickly. Bankruptcy does not mean that you will automatically be denied all credit for ten years. In fact, many firms look at bankruptcy as a responsible way of discharging debts when there is no other way out. Creditors fear bankruptcy, but they also realize that if they lend to someone who has declared bankruptcy, they need not worry about another bankruptcy for seven more years (you can only file once every seven years). If you happen to have a good explanation for the bankruptcy, such as medical bills, divorce, or some other catastrophic event, a creditor may be willing to overlook it and extend credit. Ask potential creditors about their policy toward bankruptcies. Their responses may be surprising.

A NOTE FROM THE AUTHOR

I must stress that this chapter is meant as a short overview of the bankruptcy procedure. Before filing, *at very least* you should get yourself a book devoted solely to bankruptcy. For a more complicated case, hiring an attorney, if possible, would be even more advisable. I am not an attorney and I am not, despite the research that went into this chapter, qualified to give legal advice. Do more research or consult with a professional before deciding to file. Good luck.

CHAPTER 12

THE TRUTH ABOUT LENDERS

Money lenders have sold their wares since the Age of Rome. In the Middle Ages they financed wars, put kings on thrones, and even placed a few popes in office. Almost always despised among the public—things haven't changed much—lenders have wielded incredible power since the invention of money. Even in today's computer age the anatomy of a loan stays pretty much the same. A lender supplies money, charges interest, and keeps the difference between what he pays and what he charges as a profit. The greater the risk, the more interest he charges. Money merchants today, as in years gone by, try to minimize their risk while maximizing the amount of interest charged. The careful selection of borrowers is what separates a profitable provider of credit from a bankrupt one. Modern lenders look at five criteria when granting a loan: character, capacity, collateral, capital, and conditions.

THE FIVE C'S OF LENDING

O *Character.* What kind of person is the potential creditor? Does she pay her bills? Is she stable? Loan officers love stability. The more predictable someone is, the better her chance of getting a loan. Almost all of the information gathered will come from a credit report. While creditors preach the value of the Five C's, in reality a credit report and a scoring system using the information on the application will probably be the only research utilized. The credit report, as mentioned before, includes not only credit history but current addresses, possibly your employment, and any legal action that may have resulted in judgments. The focus of the lender will be toward negative rather than positive information. Inconsistencies in the application will also be scrutinized. Character may be measured by other factors. Marital status, time on the job, and age are all factors that can affect the decision to extend credit.

○ *Capacity.* Can you afford to pay this debt? Creditors look at debt ratios (the percentage of debt payment to income) and, once again, time on the job. The kind of job is also taken into consideration. A blue-collar job in a cyclical industry such as the auto industry is less desirable than a white-collar profession such as doctor or lawyer.

○ *Collateral.* Is the loan secured or unsecured? If it is secured, how much money is being put down? A secured loan, or one backed by specific property, is obviously a much better risk than an unsecured loan, which requires a signature only. In a secured loan like a car loan or a home mortgage, the larger the down payment, the smaller the risk to the lender.

○ *Capital.* How much money do you have in the bank? What other kinds of assets do you possess? Bank accounts, stocks, bonds, and real estate all influence a credit application positively. The more outside capital a borrower has, the more inclined the lender will be to make a loan.

○ *Conditions.* Is there a recession? Is the applicant's job category becoming obsolete? In times of recession or economic downturn, creditors tighten their credit criteria by raising the requirements for loans. They may ask for more money down, require more income, or stop lending to certain kinds of professions. The current rate of interest also plays a role in determining how much money is available to lend as does the number of bad loans the lender has made in the past.

These are the formal rules of lending by which almost any banker will swear. In reality, the decision to make any loan other than a mortgage will be based almost entirely on character. Character is judged specifically by what a person has done in the past and by what people in their demographic profile tend to do. Accordingly, two pieces of information almost single-handedly determine whether a loan is made: the credit report and a credit scoring system.

THE CREDIT DECISION

The analysis of the credit report and credit scoring system together are compared to a set of minimum standards termed the "underwriting criteria," which vary from institution to institution. These minimum standards must be met before a loan can even be considered. For instance, the lending company may not lend to anyone who has had a bankruptcy or who has been on the job less than a year. Such institutional standards can only be overridden at the highest levels and could be considered part of the credit scoring system, even though a formal scoring based on points may not be needed. The criteria establish a framework within which individual underwriters can work.

Even if an application meets all of the necessary criteria, the person making the credit decision can still deny your loan because of some other factor. An underwriter is much safer denying a marginal loan than granting it. If the loan goes bad, it will cast a shadow on the underwriter's judgment. If the applicant fits the institution's idea of an ideal borrower, on the other hand, the underwriter could not be personally blamed if the candidate defaulted.

Lending models Lenders try to limit underwriters' discretion by creating lending models, or credit scoring systems, in which "points" are assigned to certain criteria. If the points add up to a certain score or higher, the creditor will consider the applicant a good credit risk. The focus of a lending model is usually on several factors:

○ *Income.* Low-income families have three times the risk of default of high-income families. The higher the income, the greater the chance of approval. This may sound obvious, but let me elaborate. A high-income person is likely to be able to carry a higher debt ratio. He will probably be allowed to borrow a larger percentage of his income than a low-income individual.

○ *Debt ratio.* Probably the most important and most heavily weighed factor in a credit scoring system. The more debt you have in proportion to your income, the greater the likelihood of default. If debts do not appear on your credit report or application, they will obviously not be included in your score.

○ *Liquid assets.* An applicant with no savings has five times the chance of default as one with $2,000 in the bank. When applying for credit, be sure to list any savings you may have at the time, including money in your checking account, even if you plan to use it during the month.

○ *Education.* A college graduate is almost three times as likely to pay his or her bills on time as a high school dropout.

○ *Home ownership.* A renter is almost twice as likely to default as a homeowner. This part of credit scoring can very greatly from city to city. In New York, for example, it may not be as important as in Des Moines.

○ *Age.* Any given age group is just as likely to default as any other, except when the applicant is over forty-five. Even then the decline in percentage of late payments does not go down substantially. A married person, however, is almost half as likely to have late payments as an unmarried person. If the applicant has children, the default ratio rises significantly.

○ *Previous turndowns.* Someone who has been denied credit by someone else is more than twice as likely to make late payments or default. Any inquiries on your credit report without corresponding lines of credit indicate a turndown to the lender.

○ *Job type.* This scores the kind of job you hold. Management titles are preferable to sales titles. Students and craftsmen score fairly high, while the self-employed and unemployed score very low. A person with a job tenure of two to three years has half the chance of missing a payment or defaulting of a person with less than two years experience. Any increase in tenure after that has a negligible affect on potential delinquency. For an example of how a credit scoring system might work, let's look at a hypothetical applicant named Larry Love. Larry is applying for a personal loan at a bank that uses a credit scoring system. His credit report is clean and he's recently applied for and received a Visa card with a small credit limit. The scoring system being used has a total of 100 points.

Job: Assistant Manager of a convenience store. Lower level management.
11 points out of a possible 15
Three years on the job: 12 points out of a possible 15

Income: $22,000 per year. Larry is in the 4th quintile of the area average, or the bottom 40 percent of all earners.
12 points out of a possible 20

Education: Didn't finish high school.
2 points out of 5

Debt ratio: Extremely low.
8 points out of 10

**Liquid
savings:** $2000 in the bank.
8 points out 10

**Home
ownership:** Rents.
3 points out of 5

Age: 24.
4 points out of 10

**Previous
turndowns:** None, recently approved for Visa card.
8 points out of 10.

The institution requires 70 points out of a 100 in order to make a loan. Larry squeaks by with a 71. This particular institution chose to value certain attributes and information more than others. It based most of its decision on income and job type. In a competitive credit environment, standards generally lower during prosperous times and rise sharply in a recession. In any type of economic environment, however, every institution will have an ideal borrower or a target market. The ideal target for the bank at which Larry applied was probably something like this:

Job: Middle or upper management
On the job more than 3 years

Income: First or second quintile in earnings (earns rnore than 60 percent of the area average)

Education: College graduate

Debt ratio: Low debt ratio

**Liquid
savings:** Liquid savings in excess of $2,000, or twice his credit limit

**Home
ownership:** Home owner

Age: Aged 35 to 45
Married, no children

**Previous
turndowns:** Solid credit history

Although Larry didn't quite fit the mold, this is probably the ideal or the mythical borrower against which all others are measured. Different institutions target different borrowers. Before applying to a particular lender , it is wise to understand to whom they are trying to market.

THE PERSONALITIES OF INSTITUTIONS

Different institutions focus on particular markets. American Express, for example, doesn't advertise in the *PennySaver*. It is more likely to target its upscale market in magazines like *Forbes* and *The New Yorker*. Some institutions, like Citibank, target a wide variety of markets. The ones that do this are usually larger institutions that are very heavily invested in consumer lending. Here are a few examples of different kinds of institutions and the markets they lend to.

Large commercial banks Citibank, Chase Manhattan, and Bank of America pursue most lending markets very aggressively. If you are establishing credit, these are especially good institutions to deal with. They lend on credit cards, student loans, automobiles, homes, and just about any other credit need. They lend to all markets, from lower to highest income. Their marketing focus includes just about everyone.

Savings and loans Remember "It's A Wonderful Life"? Savings and loans were created to be in the business of lending money on homes. Although some diversified in the 1980s, most of the more aggressive thrifts have been absorbed by the federal government or other savings and loans over the past few years. Any kind of loan other than a home loan is usually offered only as a convenience to customers. Lending criteria are ordinarily very tight, and some institutions may not even offer auto loans or personal lines of credit. Credit card rates are commonly uncompetitive and difficult to qualify for. Since most of their good customers have a higher-than-average net worth, S & L marketing efforts for consumer credit, if any, are geared toward a higher-income market.

Credit unions Who said socialism is dead? Credit unions use a brand of consumer communism that can make them excellent candidates for borrowing. They lend their own members' money to other members, operating to provide credit for those who require it. Very much like a farmer's cooperative, the unions' sole purpose is to provide financing to their own. Unfortunately, because of their size they are often limited in the number of products they can offer. Their target market is their members, whose attributes are usually determined by the kind of profession the credit union serves. Although credit standards can be tight at some institutions, these are very good places for car loans and personal lines of credit.

Finance companies Finance companies began lending money to consumers long before big banks discovered the consumer credit boom. At a time when large commercial banks provided credit only to corporations and blue-blood depositors, finance companies were lending money for cars, furniture, and other consumer needs. Charging higher rates than most banks, finance companies were also very profitable. Today, finance companies are more a lender of last resort.

Each institution has a distinct personality. By understanding the market the institution is targeting, a borrower can choose the appropriate lender and tailor his application accordingly.

GETTING TO "YES"

Appearances are extremely important in the credit business. Every underwriter working out there would like to have a good reason for making a lending decision. Most underwriters are under pressure to produce as many accepted applications as possible while limiting the number of defaults. Lenders do not want to say no. They are, afterall, in the business of lending. But if they can't find a good reason to lend to you, they won't. Tailor your application to what your lender is looking for. If you work in a record shop, don't call yourself a clerk but an assistant manager (check with your boss first in case the bank calls to confirm). Emphasize your strong points while de-emphasizing your weak points. If you are rejected on the first application, write a letter to the lending institution and ask it to reconsider. Explain why the concern named in the rejection letter (lack of credit, time on the job, etc.) is not valid. Sell yourself as a good credit risk. It is surprising how many requests for reevaluation, with explanations, result in credit being approved. Research the institution you are planning to apply to before applying. Explain any potential credit problems before you apply. Talk to an underwriter if possible, and plead your case in person. By getting an indication of how an institution will look at your application before you apply, you may very well save an inquiry on your credit report, an inquiry that could hinder your next application. The better you understand the institution you plan to deal with and its credit criteria, and the closer you can get to someone who can make a decision, the better your chances of success.

CHAPTER 13

CREDIT CARDS

Millions of charge cards have been issued to Americans. In today's fast-paced society, they have become the payment mode of choice. Almost every merchant accepts credit cards; a few are even automated. In some areas, for example, gas can be purchased by simply running your card through a slot beside the gas pump. Video tapes can be rented from a vending machine. Even grocery purchases can be charged to a credit card. We truly are becoming the cashless society. But what makes the system work? How can millions of transactions be processed and paid so quickly? How do credit card companies make money?

TURNING A PROFIT IN THE CASHLESS SOCIETY
Credit cards were invented by individual retailers. The card could only be used in the store that issued it. They made money (and still do) not only from the interest on the loans but from the sale of merchandise. Automobile companies invented auto loans for the same reason: to increase sales.

The idea of a universal credit card was a little harder to envision. Why would merchants bother accepting it? What if the balance was paid in full every month; how would the issuer make money? Convenience cards like American Express were the first to appear on the scene. They were often called travel cards and required full payment every month. Merchants signed up to increase business. If the hotel across the street accepted a travel card and you didn't, business would be lost, or so the pitch went. The only disadvantage was that every time someone charged something, a fee was assessed ranging anywhere from 2 to 5 percent. The merchant absorbed this cost. Accordingly, travel cards were usually accepted only in the more prestigious locations and in luxury-oriented stores, where higher profit margins could absorb the fees. Eventually, competition drove even lower-margin merchants to accept convenience cards. Other cards, like Mastercard and Visa, sought to grab a bigger market share by offering to finance consumer purchases and to allow monthly payments. Neither, however, was in the business of lending, or capable of producing the huge amounts of capital needed to finance such a venture (although Mastercard was originally BankAmericard, owned by Bank of America). Credit card issuers approached banks with a deal: you issue the cards, we'll keep the fee from the merchant, and you keep the interest earned from revolving balances or the unpaid balances left on credit cards at the end of each month. Banks discovered one of their most profitable consumer lending activities, and the two major credit card issuers increased sales at exponential rates. The credit age was born. Although a few upstarts have since infringed upon Visa's and Mastercard's territory, only one has had any success. Discover card, by offering reduced merchant fees and lower customer fees and by using Sears credit card holders as an initial base, soon became a third contender in what used to be the "Big Two." Others have had little luck penetrating the lucrative universal card market.

SAVING MONEY ON YOUR CREDIT CARDS

A lot of people assume that most credit cards are basically the same; they all have an annual fee and charge 19 to 21 percent interest rates. Actually, credit cards vary in costs as much as department stores, appliance stores, or auto dealerships. Which credit card or cards you should choose depends upon your credit needs. Here are some of the features you want to look at.

Interest rate Some cards offer interest rates as low as 13.5 percent fixed (Amalgamated Trust) or 10.5 percent variable (Simmons First National). These cards may not be as easy to obtain as ones with higher interest rates, but rate often has nothing to do with eligibility. Most cards with lower interest rates do not advertise or have the overhead of larger issuers. On a $2,000 balance a rate of 10.5 percent can save you $200 a year in interest costs, or almost 50 percent compared to a card charging 21 percent. If you tend to carry higher balances on your credit card, a lower interest rate may save you even more. Appendix C lists the thirty nationally-issued cards with the lowest interest rates. Call the issuers and ask for their income and credit requirements.

Annual charge Many cards have also stopped charging annual fees. Some of these issuers also offer lower-than-average interest rates on balances, making these cards even better buys. If you tend to pay off your balances in full every month, a card without an annual fee is worth looking at, even if the interest rate charged is higher.

Grace period The grace period is the amount of time some creditors allow between the time something is purchased on your credit card and when interest is charged. If you pay your balance in full every month, you should look for a card with a grace period, but if you carry a balance, a low rate of interest can more than compensate for the lack of a grace period. Appendix C lists cards with no fees and the grace period of each. Consult the lender regarding the income and credit requirements.

Departments store cards and gasoline company credit cards also offer very good values for many consumers. Although interest rates are often no bargain, most do offer grace periods and most have no annual fees. Gasoline cards do not show up on your credit bureau reports and so do not affect your debt ratio. Most gasoline cards are similar to convenience cards in that they need to be paid off at the end of the month and are often very easy to get. They usually allow payments to be made on larger purchases, such as auto repairs and tires.

Whatever kind of credit you are seeking, take some time to shop, regardless of your credit history. If you are concerned about qualifying, call up the lending institution and ask for its lending requirements. Try to talk to someone who can make the credit decision and ask whether she thinks you would qualify. Don't assume that all credit costs are the same.

CARDS FOR THOSE WITH LESS THAN PERFECT CREDIT

Several years ago some financial institutions began to notice that a growing segment of the population was unable to take advantage of their credit cards because of previous credit problems. The segment was growing at an ever-increasing rate because of the glut of credit cards on the market and the extension of credit by many banks to just about anyone with a clean credit file. Credit cards had become so essential to many functions of everyday life, like cashing a check, renting a car, or getting a hotel room, that some banks began to see a market in people who couldn't qualify for major credit cards because of their credit history. They also discovered that they could charge as much as they want and still issue a large number of credit cards. In order to secure the loan, a deposit of at least the amount of the credit line is required. The fees on the early versions of secured credit cards were astronomical, but as competition has entered the marketplace, fees have gone down and many new features have been added. Large banks like Citibank are now looking at this market, and costs may decline even further. In spite of above-average costs, secured credit cards offer several benefits to those with challenging credit other than the convenience of having a major credit card. The first benefit is an opportunity to rebuild your credit and possibly have it reflect on your credit bureau reports. The second is a good credit reference for future borrowing. As with regular credit cards a consumer should shop for those with the lowest fees, but there should also be other considerations when choosing a secured credit card.

○ *The deposit account.* The security account should be a bank savings account or an FDIC-insured certificate of deposit. Although the interest rate is not likely to be competitive, it should pay something.

○ *Credit bureau reporting.* The card company should report the status of your account to all three major credit bureaus. If it doesn't, part of the purpose for getting a secured card is defeated.

○ *Unsecured credit at later date.* Ideally, a card should refund the deposit or raise your credit limit without an additional deposit after you have paid satisfactorily for a given period, usually two years. This is an ideal circumstance, because many otherwise good cards do not offer this feature and some that do are a little more difficult to qualify for.

For more information on secured cards, see appendix C.

DEBIT CARDS

In many gas stations and grocery stores across the country, you need not have cash, checks, or a credit card to make a purchase. Simply run your ATM card through a slot, punch in your secret code and *voilà!*, the transaction is complete. Cash can be obtained over and above the purchase. In California this service is available not only in gas stations and grocery stores but fast food restaurants, gift stores, and scores of other places. Debit cards are becoming the wave of the future, and Visa and Mastercard are not about to miss the trend. Debit cards were offered by many banks several years ago, but because of the lack of computerized approval systems at most merchant locations, the risk of overcharging was substantial. In the last decade almost every merchant has obtained a credit card approval terminal, and debit cards are catching on again. Although most debit cards are not reported to credit bureaus unless you overcharge, if you are establishing credit and are looking for references to use to open instant accounts at department stores or other merchants, a debit card might be worth looking at. If you have some cash, usually a $5,000 minimum, the easiest place to open a debit card account is at a brokerage firm. Charles Schwab will give you a Mastercard debit card on its Schwab One account that will debit your brokerage account's money market account. The money market account is completely liquid, and you can write checks on it as well as buy stocks and mutual funds. No fees are charged. Other, larger brokerage firms offer similar programs.

Although most secured credit card issuers and even some debit card issuers will run a credit check, some banks will issue credit cards without a credit check. The catch is that you usually have to have a large amount of money on deposit with them. European banks, especially those in Switzerland, will issue credit cards like American Express for larger depositors, usually with a minimum of $25,000. Some American banks will do the same for even smaller deposits. I've heard of shaky savings and loans issuing Visa cards for as little as $10,000 on deposit in a term Certificate of Deposit. This is usually not a debit card or a secured line but a separate credit card. If you have some savings, ask your banker. If they don't offer such an arrangement, call around. Try smaller institutions, which may be more flexible.

SHOPPING FOR FRINGE BENEFITS

To some, credit cards are merely a convenience; to others, a method of easy financing. As credit card companies have mushroomed, however, competition has created a whole new way of differentiating companies from each other. Certain cards now offer warranties on what you purchase; others offer rebates or fringe benefits, like free frequent travel mileage. There are discounts, special tickets, and automatic rental car insurance to help lure us into using a particular issuer's plastic. Ask potential credit card issuers what kinds of special benefits they offer card holders. Call your current credit card issuer and ask what types of benefits are available to you as a current cardholder. Tell them you are considering switching companies. Some will waive the annual fee simply because you are considering getting a card that doesn't charge one. Try to negotiate. Amid growing competition, today's credit card companies are more likely than ever to give in.

Remember to use your credit card when making purchases through the mail, or when you are not assured of being satisfied with the service or product you are buying until it is purchased. If the service or product turns out to be shoddy or other than was represented, you can refuse to pay that portion of your credit card bill by writing to the credit card company and asking them to intervene. The credit card company is responsible for investigating the matter, if you notify them in writing, and cannot force you to pay until the matter has been resolved. This right is often overlooked by consumers. For more information, refer to appendix C.

Credit cards are a wonderful tool and an essential one in today's computerized society. Don't be fooled into believing it's not worth shopping around. Trying to find a credit card company that matches your needs will not only save you money but may help you avoid unnecessary headaches down the line.

CHAPTER 14

BUYING A CAR

Joe Isuzu sees you walking onto the lot. He strains to see what you drove up in.

"A late-model Toyota, not bad."

He puts on a smile and walks vigorously in your direction. You see him coming and try to stroll away, putting as many cars between him as you can. He's good. He dodges around the pickup truck and takes a short cut over the grass. You spot the bathroom. You break into a run. He sprints after you. Two other salesmen catch sight of you out of the corners of their eyes. They drop their invoices and start to chase after you. It's a Sunday morning and you're the only customer on the lot. They're all reaching into their pockets for a breath mint and a business card. Ten feet from the bathroom you run into a very large man with a gold chain and a cheap-looking tie. His name tag reads "Sales Manager" and his cup says "Most Valuable Linebacker—Western College Class of '72."

" Can I help you?" he says. You wake up in a cold sweat.

Do you know anyone who actually likes shopping for a car? Walking onto a car lot is as traumatic as trying to get financing for your new purchase, especially if you have bad credit or no credit history. Although in theory secured loans, like those used to purchase cars, are safer than unsecured loans like credit cards, financing is not necessarily easy to obtain. Unlike revolving card accounts, car loans can be loaded with arcane features that make the terms of the loan advantageous to the lender rather than the borrower. This is especially true with dealer-financed loans. In the end, shopping around will probably net you the best deal, regardless of your credit standing.

BANK FINANCING

Banks are traditionally the best source of automobile financing. Almost all bank loans use declining balance loans. This means that interest is only paid on the amount of principal currently owed and that the amount of interest paid on the loan goes down each month. For example, let's look at a $10,000 loan that is made for three years at 10% interest. The monthly payment is $322.67. In the first month, $83.33 of that payment goes towards *interest* and $239.34 toward *principal*. In the second month the balance due is now $9,760.66 ($10,000 minus $239.34) and $81.34 of the $322.67 payment goes towards *interest* and $241.33 goes towards *principal*. The balance of the loan declines, as does the amount of interest paid every month. This differs from other types of loans, such as Rule of 78 loans, in which you pay interest in the full amount of the original loan every month.

Banking institutions generally offer the lowest rates available, apart from special manufacturer rates. The rate is dependant on several factors.

○ *The amount of the down payment.* The larger it is, the lower the rate. Anything more than 30 percent, however, doesn't really influence the rate. A loan that doesn't require any money down will usually have a higher interest rate. Most loans require 10 to 20 percent, unless your credit rating and income level are exceptionally good.

○ *The length of time to finance.* The shorter, the better. A three-year loan will probably have a better rate than a seven-year loan (usually only available for luxury cars).

○ *The kind of car.* Loans on higher-priced cars often have correspondingly higher interest rates because of the large amount of money being borrowed. The potential for depreciation will also be taken into account by the lender. A lower-priced car can hold its value better because it is easier to sell. Some luxury cars, such as Mercedes, retain their value over time. These factors may be reflected in the loan by the interest rate.

○ *Credit history.* As always, repayment history is an important part of loan application. Poor credit will result in a higher interest rate. Banks do not want to lend to someone whose credit history is extremely bad, although lending policies may vary from bank to bank. Some banks do specialize in lending to "higher risk" borrowers. Call for underwriting criteria before you apply.

If you can qualify for bank financing, look no further. Check your paper or call around for the best rates. If your credit history, or lack of credit history, prevents you from using these sources, financing is still possible. Unfortunately, it will be more expensive than financing through a more traditional source.

FINANCE COMPANIES

If the banks have turned you down, a finance company might be the next stop. Finance companies often lend to those who have been turned down at a bank. They have greater faith in their ability to collect consumer loans than larger institutions. Since most finance companies have many small offices, usually close to where their borrowers live, personal contact with borrowers is more common. If a borrower stops sending in payments, they can collect by dropping by the house and visiting in person, something very few large banks are able to do. Although they charge a higher rate of interest, finance companies will usually be cheaper than most dealer financing.

DEALER FINANCING

"WE FINANCE ANYBODY," an ad proclaims in the Los Angeles Times. "WE CARRY OUR OWN PAPER," exclaims another. Dealer financing allows, in the words of a car salesman, "anyone with a heartbeat and a down payment" to buy a car. How can dealers do this? Don't they lose money? On the contrary, in-house financing is so lucrative that one dealer in the Los Angeles area pays salesmen $100 for each referral. Dealer financing usually requires a credit check, just like any other loan. The worse an applicant's credit report is , the larger the down payment the dealer will require. The dealer will also put a premium into the price and most likely set up what is called a "Rule of 78" financing contract. Here is how the premium works: if someone wants to buy a car that usually costs $8,000, the dealer may insist on charging $10,000, a 20 percent premium. The premium may be hidden as the difference between the list price and the price the car could be negotiated down to if outside financing were available. In other words, the buyer financing the car through the dealer would pay list price, while everyone else could negotiate the price down. Some banks will finance people with bad credit by paying the dealer only 90 percent of the contract's value. If the dealer sold a car for $12,000, took in $2,000 as a down payment, and financed $10,000, the bank would pay only $9,000 for the loan. The dealer would have to absorb the $1,000 difference, and the consumer would have to pay it to the bank. This would amount to a 10 percent instant profit to the bank, if it could collect the loan. These loans are only available through dealers. The total down payment required is usually 30 percent or more, and a premium is paid either to the dealer or to the bank. Interest rates would range from 15 to 21 percent. Unlike most bank loans, the amount of interest paid would not go down every month. This is a Rule of 78 loan. If you borrowed $10,000 from a bank at 10 percent and your monthly payment was $322.67 on a three-year loan, $83.33 of your first month's payment would be interest. On the next payment only $81.34 of your payment would go toward interest, because you had paid off $239.34 in principal, meaning that the interest charged would go down. In a Rule of 78 loan the total interest is calculated up-front and full interest is paid on the original principal balance each month. In other words, you pay interest every month on the entire $10,000 loan amount. The balance used to calculate your monthly interest does not decline every month, as do most bank auto loans. This results in a higher payment for the Rule of 78 loans. For example, the payments on a Rule of 78 loan on $10,000 at 10 percent for three years would be $361.11, or $38.44 more per month than the declining balance loan. Interest would be paid on the full balance every month even though principal had been paid on the loan. Although the Rule of 78 is not a good deal, it is sometimes the only option available to those with a bad credit history. If the only choice for financing is a dealer, the buyer can always try to negotiate better terms. The dealer wants to make a deal, and he may lower the premium or the interest rate. The next time you buy a car it may be possible to get a better deal by showing the dealer that your repayment history to him has been good in the past. Automobile manufacturer's financing arms, such as Ford Motor Credit, also offer loans to those with substandard credit histories. Although these loans are more difficult to obtain than many dealer-financed loans, they do not charge premiums and do appear as part of your credit history (many dealer-sponsored loans do not).

There are a variety of dealers who carry their own paper. Look in your local newspaper's automobile section. Many dealers do not advertise these kinds of loans, so it may be wise to call around. Know the kind of contract you're making before you sign the papers, and remember, it never hurts to ask for better terms.

AUTO BROKERS

Automobile brokers make a living from being able to get a buyer any kind of car he wants, in any color, at a fleet price. No shopping, no haggling, no salesman. The fleet price is usually about as good as anyone could negotiate on his own, minus a commission for the broker.

Brokers have also begun to connect with various sources of financing, some of which lend to those with less than perfect, or even exceedingly poor, credit histories. Some of these lenders offer loans similar to dealer loans, and others offer creative leasing contracts. Since the price of the vehicle is usually better than what a dealer would offer (dealers often use their financing as leverage to get you to pay full price or better), an auto brokerage company may be a good place to shop for a new car. As with any other loan, be sure you understand the financing before you make a deal. There are some very tricky contracts, especially when it comes to leases.

LEASING

Leasing became the yuppie financing of choice in the eighties for a number of reasons. Since leases require little or nothing down, buyers can generally buy a more expensive car for less money. Payments are also lower, especially for luxury cars that hold their value well. The car is owned by the bank, which leases it to the consumer. The bank or finance company projects what the car will be worth at the end of the lease period and calculates the lease payment accordingly. The better the particular make of car has held its value in the past, the lower the payment. The person leasing the car is allowed a fixed number of miles per year and must return the car in good condition. These requirements are also factored into the lease payment. If the mileage is more than a fixed amount, or if the car is damaged, the lessee (the car buyer) must pay the bank or finance company accordingly. There are two kinds of leases: open-ended leases and close-ended leases. An open-end lease allows the bank to calculate the value of the car at the end of the lease period and assess the lessee accordingly. If a BMW doesn't turn out to hold its value as well as estimated, the lessee gets a bill. A closed-end lease requires the lender to guarantee a residual value at the end of the lease. Regardless of what the fair market value is, the borrower is not assessed any charges based on the market value of the car. The closed-end lease is generally a better deal for the buyer. A lessee can usually pay the lender the residual value—that is, the value of the car at the end of the lease—and own the car. This is called "buying out the lease," and most leases offer this option. Although leasing usually requires very good credit and past auto loans, some lenders, many through auto brokers, are offering leasing for customers with poor credit. A lease sometimes called an "Equi-lease" is used to entice borrowers. As with many other leases, only the first and last month's payment and a small security deposit are usually required. The residual value of the car is purposely set very low so that the monthly payments are quite a bit higher. At the end of the lease the buyer has the choice of coming up with the residual in cash or turning the car over to the bank, which will easily resell it at a higher price than the residual. When the rate of interest is calculated on this kind of lease, it turns out to be quite high but still much lower than some of the purchase contracts offered by dealers. Each lease would have to be considered carefully on its own terms. Many auto brokers advertise in the classified section of newspapers or in community newspapers. Remember that leases do not have the same repossession requirements as auto loans. If the car is taken back on a lease, it may not be able to be redeemed as easily as a car repossessed for a delinquent auto loan. Check your lease agreement and your state laws for more information.

AUTO LOAN RIP-OFFS

As the recession deepens, con artists seem to be popping up everywhere. One of the biggest and most popular rip-offs involves "taking over someone's payments." Many so-called auto brokers advertise "auto loans with no credit check" in local newspapers. In the same newspaper they offer to take over payments on existing auto loans. By putting together those needing a car and those wanting to get rid of one, auto brokers perform what seems to be a needed service: the buyer makes the payments and keeps the car, and the seller rids themselves of unaffordable payments. Of course, a fee is taken by the broker in the form of a "downpayment." Unfortunately, this seemingly innocuous exchange is not all that it appears. There are several problems that both buyer and seller will probably face at a later time.

- If the bank finds out about the exchange they will call the loan. In other words, they will demand full payment on the balance due. The buyer will be out any money he has put into the transaction, and the seller will be responsible for the balance of the loan.

- The original owner of the car is ultimately responsible for the payments. The payment history of the buyer will appear on the seller's credit history because, technically, they still own the car.

- After the buyer has made the payments, the original owner may decide not to give up ownership of the car. The buyer may have a written contract, but he will have to go to court to enforce it. The car may be sold by the time the matter is settled.

○ If the original owner has a poor driving record, the buyer may have to pay higher insurance rates. The original owner must be kept on the insurance because records of the auto insurance must go to the bank holding the loan. Insurance companies will probably not insure a vehicle without some proof of ownership.

Auto brokers will make many claims. The most outrageous one is that after a few months of making payments the bank will transfer the loan into the new buyer's name. Not so. Most banks say that such an exchange can only occur through the regular credit process. A person taking over another's payments would not be any more likely to qualify than if they had applied on their own. Beware of "auto brokers." In many states such businesses are prohibited by law. Don't be taken in.

If you do plan to take over someone's payments, consider doing it only if both parties know each other well. If an old friend, family member, or other known quantity is involved, the arrangement may be successful.

Another rip-off that is becoming popular is the "loan broker" scam. Advertising, again, in newspapers, these "brokers" claim to be able to locate private sources of money for a fee. As you might guess, the location fee is never seen after it has been paid, and after enough complaints have been filed, the "broker" simply closes up shop and starts over again in another town. If it sounds too good to be true, it probably is. If you have bad credit, don't expect anyone to extend you an unsecured loan at a low rate. Bad credit may not end your chances of obtaining financing, but you will have to pay more than someone with perfect credit.

Even those with the worst credit can get financed when buying a car. Take the time to talk to lenders. It may be surprising how many are willing to work with you. Don't be afraid to ask questions and negotiate. You can save a substantial amount of money and a lot of headaches.

CHAPTER 15

FINANCING REAL ESTATE

Home ownership is part of the 'American dream. Some might even call it a right. Over 64 percent of Americans own their own homes, a far greater percentage than almost any other western nation. For years Congress has encouraged individual home ownership by creating and preserving institutions devoted solely to issuing home loans. Government agencies buy and sell home mortgages, creating a market for home loans that meet their criteria. These criteria usually include a certain debt ratio, a minimum down payment, a fairly good credit history, and a limited size of loan. Loans meeting the United States government agency requirements are called "conforming loans." Although many lenders focus on government agency criteria, there are other lenders who treat mortgages as investments, which they hold themselves or sell to private investors. Loans not purchased by a government agency are called non-conforming loans. Most real estate loans, regardless of their ultimate destination, are subject to similar standards.

THE APPLICATION PROCESS—WHAT LENDERS LOOK FOR
Lenders take five factors into account during the application process:

Income Can the borrower afford the payments? Most lenders will want to see two years of income history. The longer someone has been at her present job or in the same line of work, the better. Income from commission or self-employment will be treated with suspicion, and additional documentation will usually be required to verify income. Lenders have recently been raising their income expectations (and other criteria) in response to losses in real estate lending. Showing as much income as possible can only help the application. Certain loans involving larger down payments (over 30 percent) are known as no-qualifiers.

They do not require any income qualification, but, in a tight credit environment, are becoming harder to find and much more expensive.

Debt ratio There are actually two parts to a debt ratio: the housing ratio, which is the percentage of income taken up by housing expenses, and total debt ratio, which includes all monthly payments on housing and other debts combined. These ratios are calculated by adding up all monthly payments (or just the housing expense costs in the case of the housing ratio) and dividing them by total income, before taxes. Many government agencies that purchase mortgages from lenders require certain percentages, which the lenders (acting, in effect, as brokers) pass on to borrowers. If a government agency requires a housing ratio lower than 28 percent and a debt ratio lower than 36 percent, the lender may require the same. The bank can then sell its loans and re-lend again, pocketing the fees, or points. A conforming loan is limited to a certain size, typically around $192,500. In some parts of the country, like Southern California or New York, loans tend to be larger. Since there are no rules for debt ratios on non-conforming loans, lenders can set the parameters based on experience or current lending policy. If a lower down payment is involved, a lower housing and debt ratio will usually be required.

Credit history Credit problems do not disqualify you from traditional sources of mortgages, such as banks or savings & loans. If the problem is older and was resolved, it may not effect the loan application process. One or two negative items on a credit report alongside several positive ones might easily be explained away. Perhaps the applicant went through a divorce or had to cope with extraordinary hospital bills. Check the lender's policy on credit before applying. Even the most conservative lenders can be surprisingly accommodating to those with marginal credit histories. Some of the most cautious savings and loans will lend to people who have declared bankruptcy as long as it was discharged more than three years ago. The decision to overlook negative credit is always based on the circumstances of the problem. An explanation to the loan officer before applying will often uncover the lender's policy on negative credit.

Property appraisal The institution granting the mortgage will probably not take your word as to the value of the property. They will want it appraised independently or by an appraiser in their employ. The value affixed to the house depends on a variety of factors, such as the appraiser's particular disposition that day and his or her prior experience.

Source of cash for down payment Lenders want to be sure they know where all of the cash for the down payment is coming from. A minimum of 5 percent of the buyer's available cash is usually required. The remainder can come from the seller carrying a second mortgage (more on that later), a gift from a family member, or the proceeds of a retirement plan. They will insist on proof that the money has been in the bank for a few months (bank statements, etc). In the recent credit crunch many lenders are also requiring proof of three months' worth of expenses in current savings. If the recession grows deeper, these lending requirements may tighten up even more.

Every lender tries to quantify its lending formula to separate good credit risks from bad ones Part of the trick in securing a loan is to know as much about the formula as possible and then choose a lender most likely to lend to someone like you. The second important factor is to choose the kind of loan that bests suits your needs.

KINDS OF MORTGAGES

There are several different categories of mortgages. Two already mentioned are conforming and non-conforming. A conforming mortgage meets the guidelines of a mortgage that can be sold to a government agency such as FHLMC (Federal Home Loan Mortgage Corporation) or FNMA (Federal National Mortgage Association). The lender is no longer responsible for the debt once the mortgage is sold. A non-conforming loan does not meet federal guidelines and as a result is subject to higher interest rates. Borrowers are also given the choice of a fixed or an adjustable-rate loan. A fixed-rate mortgage carries the same interest rate during the entire life of the loan, while an adjustable rate adjusts every six months or so. Fixed-rate borrowers pay the same amount every month. The payments on an adjustable rate mortgage are adjusted periodically according to current interest rates. The interest rate is usually determined as a percentage of a published rate, such as the cost of funds in a certain federal reserve district, or treasury bond rates. In addition to paying interest, borrowers often pay a fee up front called "points." These points (each point is equivalent to 1 percent of the loan value) go to pay the commissions of the loan officer or broker and toward the overhead and profit of the lending institution. Fixed-rate loans have recently been quite popular because of lower interest rates. There are several kinds of fixed-rate loans.

Government loans The FHA and the VA (Federal Housing Association and the Veterans Administration) offer special loans to those who qualify. Down-payment requirements are usually low, as are interest rates. Both offer thirty-year or fifteen-year fixed loans. The FHA rates are customarily a half-point lower than a regular loan (.5 percent), and the loan is much easier to qualify for than conventional mortgages. The down payment is anywhere from 3 to 5 percent. FHA loan amounts are lower, and an up-front fee equivalent to 3.8 points is charged.

VA loans are available only to veterans, active servicemen, and the unmarried widows of veterans. The maximum loan amount is $135,000, and loans without down payments are offered ($110,000 maximum). Only one point in fees is assessed.

Jumbo mortgages A jumbo mortgage is any mortgage that does not conform with the limits on loan size imposed by FNMA and FHLMC. Although jumbo loans are uncommon in many parts of the country because of lower home prices, in higher-priced urban areas such as San Francisco and New York they are more common than conforming loans. A jumbo loan frequently has a higher rate of interest and tighter credit and debt ratio requirements.

Fifteen-year mortgages Traditional fixed-rate mortgages are thirty years long. During the early years of the loan, almost the entire payment is consumed by interest. As the loan ages, a progressively lower portion of the payment is interest and a higher percentage goes toward repayment of principal. A fifteen-year mortgage has a slightly higher payment than a traditional mortgage but pays off principal much more quickly. The interest rate is usually lower because of the shorter repayment period. Take the example of a $100,000 loan. A thirty-year fixed loan at 10 percent would have a monthly payment of $877.57. A fifteen-year loan at 9.75 percent would have a payment of $1,059.36, only 20 percent higher. Yet after ten years, the thirty-year mortgage would still have a $90,000 balance owing, while the fifteen-year mortgage would have a balance due of only $50,000. Over the life of the loan the thirty-year mortgage holder would have paid a total of $215,926 in interest, while the fifteen-year mortgage holder would have paid only $90,685 in interest. While the savings can be substantial, qualifying can also be much more difficult, because of the higher payment.

Buydowns A buydown is often used to make a loan easier to qualify for by lowering the interest rate. In exchange, the lender will charge more points for the loan. A permanent buydown locks in a given interest rate during the entire length of the loan. A temporary buydown is the kind most often used in getting home owners qualified more easily. The two most popular temporary buydowns are 2-1 buydowns and 3-2-1 buy downs. A 2-1 buydown is a loan where the interest rate is reduced by 2 percentage points the first year and 1 the second. For example, a lender is offering a thirty-year fixed loan at 10 percent. It may offer the loan as a 2-1 buydown by charging 8 percent the first year, 9 percent the second, and 10 percent the third. It compensates for the initially lower interest rate by charging more points up front or by setting the final rate slightly higher than the market. The buyer can qualify more easily for the loan and the lender is able to accomplish its goal of lending money.

Adjustable-rate mortgages In the early 1980's, many savings and loans faced insolvency. The government had lifted regulations limiting the amount that could be paid on bank accounts, at about the same time that interest rates were going through the ceiling. As a result, banks were holding mortgages that were paying 5 to 8 percent while they were forced to pay depositors 16 percent or better on their bank accounts. Congress reacted by allowing savings and loans to invest in junk bonds and commercial real estate, while several astute industry executives dealt with the dilemma by creating a new kind of mortgage, the adjustable-rate mortgage. They reasoned that no one would want to lock in a fixed rate at 20 percent or better, so why not offer a mortgage that adjusts with interest rates? Lenders would never again run the risk of having to borrow short term at a higher rate than they were getting on their long-term investments, namely home mortgages. Although adjustable rate mortgages usually offer lower rates, and thus easier qualification, than fixed mortgages, they are not suited for the faint of heart. An unusually large hike in interest rates, for example, could drastically increase a mortgage payment. Many adjustable rate loans try to mitigate this risk by capping the amount that a payment can rise. Unfortunately, this may lead to negative amortization, when the payment made does not cover the interest due and the principal balance of the loan rises rather than falls. When you are shopping for adjustable-rate loans, certain features should be included in the loan to offset the effects of negative amortization. One of these features might be a loan with a lifetime interest rate cap. This feature limits the amount the interest rate can rise by capping the amount the lender can charge during the life of the loan. A convertibility feature can also help by allowing the borrower to convert to a fixed-rate loan. Although potentially easier to get, borrowers should be very cautious when considering an adjustable-rate loan.

REFINANCING
Refinancing usually involves one of two things; taking advantage

of a lower interest rate or taking money out of a house that has increased in value. Refinancing to lower interest expenses almost always involves getting a new first mortgage, which isn't really any different from getting a new mortgage. Refinancing to take cash out, on the other hand, is a whole different ballgame. For some reason, lenders are wary of home owners taking cash out when getting a new first mortgage. Perhaps they think the borrower knows something that they don't. The lending requirements are usually quite stringent on a new first with cash out. Unless a large amount is needed, it may be more economical to use a second mortgage. A second mortgage is a loan secured by the value of real estate after the first mortgage claims have been paid. Second mortgages are very popular for refinancing or acquiring new consumer debt, since the interest (unlike with consumer loans) is deductible on a borrower's income tax return. Seconds take two forms, a fixed-term, fixed-dollar amount loan or an equity line of credit. The fixed-dollar second is much like a first mortgage in that a certain dollar amount is borrowed, payments are made monthly, and the loan is repaid over a specified period of time. An equity line of credit is more like a credit card attached to your house, allowing you to write checks and take money out. You can also choose between making a minimum payment every month or paying back the entire amount. The line of credit remains open and the interest is usually deductible. Interest rates on second mortgages are almost always higher than on first mortgages. Those on lines of credit are usually higher than on fixed second loans but still much lower than credit cards.

SOURCES OF FINANCING

Real estate lending is big business. Up until the recent recession, almost everyone wanted to get into this lucrative market. Lending criteria have tightened greatly over the past few months, however, as the recession deepens and real estate prices in some formerly recession-proof areas continue to slide. Although it may be more difficult to obtain a loan than it was a year ago (especially if you have had credit problems or have no credit), it is still possible. There are four sources of traditional financing:

○ Savings and loans

○ Banks

○ Mortgage brokers

○ Private investors

Savings and loans Savings and loans lend the lion's share of money to the residential real estate market. They also have some of the toughest lending criteria. One West Coast savings and loan requires three credit relationships, including a major credit card with a higher balance. They will not accept more than one account thirty days late without a very good explanation. Yet this same institution would lend to someone with a bankruptcy as long as it was older than three years. There is often no method to these underwriting criteria, but in general, savings and loans—especially after the bailout and accompanying publicity—are very hesitant to lend to any but the most credit-worthy customers. This may not be true of a faltering institution, which may be more anxious to bring in loan fees. As with any other kind of credit, it is important to shop around and ask for underwriting criteria before filling out an application.

Banks Banks, believe it or not, tend to be a little more flexible than S & L's. Banks are generally better capitalized than thrifts and have more experience lending on riskier ventures. This is especially true of consumer-oriented banks like CitiBank, Bank of America, and Chase Manhattan. All of these banks aggressively seek new markets and are more likely than other institutions to have more progressive programs. Like the S & L's, unfortunately, banks have also been burned quite badly in real estate loans and are choosier about whom they lend to than they were a year ago. If you have any of the following problems, you may not qualify for a savings and loan or bank mortgage until you clean up your credit or a little more time passes.

- ○ A recent bankruptcy without a very good explanation. Good explanations might include loss of job, illness, catastrophic event. Bad explanations would be "I spent more money than I made" or "I took on too much debt."

- ○ Recent charge-offs, accounts over sixty days late (more than one), judgments, repossessions, foreclosures. Unless there are only one or two such accounts and a lot of other good credit, you probably won't be able to get a loan without a cosigner.

If only one or two accounts are negative and a lot of others aren't, don't despair. A detailed, plausible explanation will probably get you the loan. The same is true if credit problems occurred over a short, specific time frame. A credit report showing consistently late payments over a long period of time, however, can torpedo a loan very quickly. Mortgages can be obtained, even with bad credit, although the terms will probably be restrictive and the interest rates and points very high.

Mortgage brokers and "hard money lenders" Mortgage brokers have a very bad reputation, often with good cause. Mortgage brokers find loans for borrowers, taking a fee for their services. There are really only two reasons why you would ever want to use a mortgage broker. The first is that you truly don't have the time or the desire to shop around for rates and terms yourself. The second is that you don't qualify for a loan through traditional sources. There are a few mortgage brokers who deal only with the first kind of customer. They obtain their loans through savings and loans and banks and consider their job to be that of an advisor to real estate buyers. They find the cheapest financing and keep a close watch on the mortgage market, selling their services for a fee. Many other mortgage brokers supplement these services by offering services to those with bad credit or other qualifying problems. Some even specialize in problem loans. The services of these specialists range from obtaining financing from non-traditional sources to cleaning up a credit problem. Some brokers work in gray areas of the law and are of questionable character. Yet they do get results. One broker actually employs a third party (probably a private detective) to contact creditors and offer settlements in return for a clean credit record on that particular account. He cleans up a client's credit before he obtains a loan. Others are simply deceitful, advising borrowers to put down false information on their applications. Remember, you are the one submitting the application and the one who could face fraud charges. You are the one who could have a bankruptcy debt made non-dischargeable because of the false statements. The broker risks little compared to that.

Hard money lenders can be mortgage brokers themselves or can work in connection with mortgage brokers. These are lenders of last resort in the mortgage community. They will lend to anyone provided the down payment and/or the rate is high enough. Their terms are generally shorter, the better to protect their loan, and the up-front charges can be as high as ten points or 10 percent of the face value of the loan, depending on the circumstances. They will lend on firsts, seconds, thirds, or even fourths. They usually obtain their money from private investors, sometimes selling the loans to investors and keeping a percentage of interest and the points. Investors can include anyone from a retired real estate investor who buys trust deeds to a large corporation. Be sure to exhaust your other options before using a hard money lender.

CREATIVE FINANCING

Even if all the banks in your area have turned you down and you simply can't bring yourself to do business with a hard money lender (or can't afford the expenses), you are not relegated to renting all of your life. A little creativity and some persistence can still land you in a home. Creative financing involves the use of non-conventional financing or the use of conventional financing in a non-conventional way. If you have a weak credit history, this may be one of the best ways to obtain financing. Here are a few options.

Owner carried mortgage   The seller of a house may carry a second mortgage or even a first to help speed the sale of the house. In effect, she lends the money to the buyer. Why would she want to do this? This kind of financing usually becomes popular in a tight real estate market. Houses are moving slowly and the owner offers financing in order to move the house. The most common offer is a second. With an owner-carried second, a buyer can usually qualify for a 80/20 loan (80 percent financed, 20 percent down) at a bank and have the owner finance 15 percent. The buyer, who only has to put down 5 percent, gets a better loan with a lower rate and easier requirements than if he had tried to borrow the entire 95 percent (95 percent loans are rarely approved in the current economic environment). An owner may even carry a large first, but she must have enough equity in the house to do this. Although a desperate, cash-starved seller may be able to carry a second, she will seldom be able to carry a first. The kind of seller who carries a first is usually an older real estate investor close to retirement or a retired person trying to sell an outgrown house. When you are looking at property, try to find out who the owner is and what her circumstances are. Often a retired owner would much rather earn 9 percent on a first trust deed on her own house than get 5 percent in a bank certificate of deposit. A lower down payment can often be negotiated. Since this is a private transaction, there are no points and the terms can be anything the two parties agree upon. Such an arrangement can be ideal for a first-time buyer, but a lot of time and patience are required. Most sellers will not have considered the idea until it is presented to them. Start with privately advertised homes (no real estate agent) and present the idea to the seller if her situation looks favorable.

Equity sharing   Equity sharing has become extremely popular as housing costs have soared in many areas of the country. Although there are several variations on this arrangement, here is how an equity share basically works. A buyer finds a house but lacks the down payment to purchase it. His income is good and his credit is sound. An investor puts up the down payment in return for half of the equity in the house (the value after the loan has been paid). The buyer takes responsibility for taxes and all other payments in return for the other half. The agreement usually expires after a certain period of time, at which point the two parties can either end the agreement by having one party buy the other out, or choose to extend it. Other variations can include higher or lower percentages of equity based on the size of the down payment or other special factors. Equity shares can also be combined with an owner-financed purchase to create a nothing-down transaction. The greatest hazard with equity shares is disagreement between the partners. Many companies now offer equity-share financing from private investors, and this can intensify the problem. A great deal can go wrong when you are dealing with someone you don't know. What if the buyer wants to renovate and the investor doesn't want to put more money in? Who pays, and how does it affect the equity? I've also seen many buyers ripped off with bad equity share agreements. Perhaps the seller gives only a 25 percent equity share in exchange for monthly payments. Perhaps the transaction is only in contract form and the buyer is never on the title. The former owner mortgages the property and loses it, leaving the buyer in a losing position. There are some very good books out on equity sharing. All in all, it is probably best to enter this kind of arrangement with someone you really know, like a relative, and to make the contract as specific as possible.

Lease options Lease options are a great alternative to renting. Although the tax advantages of home ownership stay with the seller, the buyer has a chance to build equity without taking any risk in owning the property. A lease option is simply a lease on a house with the option to buy at a future time period, usually at a fixed price. The rent is often higher than the typical rent on a straight lease, but a percentage of the payment is usually applied to the down payment. Here's how a typical lease option arrangement works. The seller leases out a house with an option to buy in two years at $150,000. The buyer pays $1,250 per month in rent, which is about $150 above the market rate for a similar house. Half of the rent is applied to the down payment. After two years the buyer has $15,000 applied to the down payment, or ten percent of the value of the house. If the house has appreciated 10 percent to $165,000, she also has a $15,000 gain. Why would a seller want to use a lease option? Once again, if the real estate market is very slow, the seller may be having trouble selling the property. Perhaps he is under a time constraint, or worse, he could be desperate. The desperate ones are dangerous, and precautions are needed. If you have nothing but a lease-option contract and the property is foreclosed on, you are usually out of luck, unless you can negotiate something with the lender (good luck). When looking at a lease option, try to get your name on the title. Even if you have to pay $1,500, in the case of our previous example, to have 1 percent of the property put in your name, the fees involved to change title would be well spent. If something goes wrong, at least you'll know about it. Check out the seller carefully; make sure he is a reputable person who has been around for a while. You would also be wise to have a real estate attorney of your choosing draw up the contract or review the one given to you.

Assuming a mortgage   A seller may have an assumable mortgage, often at a very competitive rate. Some of these older mortgages do not require any qualifying. By taking over an older mortgage and having the seller carry a second mortgage, you can purchase a house with a very small down payment. VA and FHA loans are often assumable.

Co-signer   Although an equity share may work better, many people who have had credit problems or who have higher debt ratios use co-signers to secure their first piece of property. The co-signer is usually someone who trusts the borrower implicitly, since that person takes on the entire liability in the event of default and also shares the credit history of the obligation. The mortgage also affects his debt ratio. Parents, siblings, and rich uncles work best.

Many of these creative techniques can also be used in combination. Lease options, for example, can be set up to give a buyer half the equity in a home in return for making mortgage payments for three years. Owner-carried loans can be combined with equity sharing to buy out a property at the end of the equity share agreement. Let your imagination go wild. In any private transaction, however, do be sure to ask yourself these questions:

○ *How am I protected if the other party does not fulfill her part of the agreement?* Having yourself on title or having a lien against the property are the only sure ways of protecting yourself. Sellers are sometimes hesitant to agree to this.

○ *Do I trust this person?* Is this the kind of person I want to do business with? If you get a bad feeling, walk away.

If you have had credit problems, don't feel you must take whatever kind of deal you can get. People who have had credit difficulties buy real estate every day. Don't relegate yourself to the status of victim. People make mistakes all the time, and if someone doesn't want to deal with you because of your past mistakes, or insists on an obviously unfair-deal because of your credit history, go elsewhere. There will always be other people to work with.

CHAPTER 16

CREDIT SCAMS: LET THE BUYER BEWARE

"ERASE BAD CREDIT!"

"BASED ON LITTLE-KNOWN LOOPHOLES IN FEDERAL CREDIT LAWS, WE CAN SHOW YOU HOW TO CLEAN UP YOUR CREDIT REPORT!"

"MASTERCARD! VISA! REGARDLESS OF CREDIT HISTORY."

The check is in the mail. It won't cost you a dime. It was like that when I got here.

In the classified section on a given Sunday, ads can be found in almost any large newspaper across the nation, advertising a miracle: Your credit will be fixed, no strings attached. Following on the heels of the credit boom, credit repair companies have sprung up across the country. These financial carpetbaggers take advantage of consumers with poor credit histories, promising to make their financial problems go away in one fell swoop. Charging anywhere from $50 to $1,500, credit consultants do nothing that a well-informed consumer cannot do for themselves. The "modus operandi" of most credit clinics is the same. First the "credit consultant" has the customer bring in a copy of their credit report. Second, a series of letters is sent to the credit bureaus disputing all negative items. The credit bureaus are required to investigate the dispute, and if they cannot confirm the items, or the creditor does not respond, the items are removed. Sound familiar? Unlike a credit repair clinic, the procedure outlined in Chapter 4 costs nothing. Credit clinics vary in sophistication, and many border on the illegal. They may charge fees for a variety of "services," from issuing credit cards to finding auto loans. Most of these loans can be obtained by a consumer on their own without any cost. In fact, many issuers of secured credit cards refuse to send applications to credit clinics because of past abuses. The credit reporting industry has responded to the rise of credit clinics in a rather interesting way: a public relations push to "expose" the abuses of the credit clinics. Normally publicity-shy credit bureau executives appear on radio talk shows and in newspaper interviews, offering consumer tips on choosing a credit clinic. Always quick to defend the consumer, the credit industry never fails to warn consumers of credit clinic rip-offs and to stress that credit cleanup doesn't usually work. This just isn't true. Although credit clinics often charge outrageous fees and sometimes engage in outright fraud, some of their techniques do work. Don't be fooled by either side. Save your money but don't be afraid to take on a credit bureau or a creditor. After all, your ability to borrow is an asset worth protecting.

APPENDIX A

FEDERAL AND STATE AGENCY ADDRESSES

Federal Trade Commission Regional Offices.

Atlanta
(AL, FL, GA, MS, NC,
SC, TN, VA)
Federal Trade Commission
1718 Peachtree St. N.W. Rm. 1000
Atlanta, GA 30367
(404) 881-4836

Boston
(CT, ME, MA,
NH, RI, VT)
Federal Trade Commission
150 Causeway St. Rm. 1301
Boston, MA 02114
(617) 223-6621

Chicago
(IL, IN, IA, KY, MN,
MO, WI)
Federal Trade Commission
55 E. Monroe St., Suite 1437
Chicago, Ill. 60603
(312) 353-4423

Cleveland
(DE, MD, MI, OH,
PA, WV)
Federal Trade Commission
Mall Bldg., Suite 500
118 St. Clair Ave.
Cleveland, OH 44114
(216) 522-4207

Dallas
(AK, LA, NM, OK, TX)
Federal Trade Commission
8303 Elmbrook Dr.
Dallas, TX 75247
(214) 767-7050

Denver
(CO, KS, MT, NE, ND,
SD, UT, WY)
Federal Trade Commission
1405 Curtis St. Ste. 2900
Denver, CO 80202
(303) 844-2271

Los Angeles
(AZ, southern CA)
Federal Trade Commission
11000 Wilshire Blvd.
Los Angeles, CA 90024
(213) 824-7575

New York
(NJ, NY)
Federal Trade Commission
Federal Bldg. Rm. 2243-EB
26 Federal Plaza
New York, NY 10278
(212) 264-1207

San Francisco
(northern CA, Hawaii, NV)
Federal Trade Commission
450 Golden Gate Ave. Rm. 12470
San Francisco, CA 94102
(808) 546-5685
(206) 442-4655

Seattle
(AL, ID, OR, WA)
Federal Trade Commission
Federal Bldg., 28th Floor
915 Second Ave.
Seattle, WA 98174

State Attorney General's Offices
Address all inquiries to "Office of the Attorney General"

Alabama
11 S. Union St.
Montgomery, AL 36130
(205) 242-7300

Alaska
Dept. of Law
P.O. Box K
Juneau, AK 99811
(907) 465-3600

Arizona
1275 W. Washington
Phoenix, AR 85007
(602) 542-4266

Arkansas
323 Center #200
Little Rock, AR 72201
(501) 682-2007

California
1515 "K" St. Law Library
Sacramento, CA 95814
(916) 324-5437

Colorado
1525 Sherman St., 3rd Fl.
Denver, CO 80203
(303) 866-5005

Connecticut
55 Elm St.
Hartford, CT 06016
(203) 566-2026

Delaware
820 N. French St.
Wilmington, DE 19801
(302) 571-2500

Florida
The Capitol
Tallahassee, FL 32399
(904) 487-1963

Georgia
132 State Judicial Bldg.
Atlanta, GA 30334
(404) 656-4585

Hawaii
State Capitol
Honolulu, HI 96813
(808) 548-4740

Idaho
State Capitol
Boise, ID 83720
(208) 334-2400

Illinois
500 S. Second St.
Springfield, IL 62706
(217) 782-1090

Indiana
219 State House
Indianapolis, IN 46204
(317) 232-6201

Iowa
Hoover State Off. Bldg.
Des Moines, IA 50319
(515) 281-8373

Kansas
Judicial Center
Topeka, KS 66612
(913) 296-2215

Kentucky
State Capitol, Rm. 116
Frankfort, KY 40601
(502) 564-7600

Louisiana
Dept. of Justice
P.O. Box 94005
Baton Rouge, LA 70804
(504) 342-7013

Maine
State House Station #6
Augusta, ME 04333
(207) 289-3661

Maryland
7 N. Calvert St.
Baltimore, MD 21202
(301)576-6300

Massachusetts
1 Ashburton Pl.
Boston, MA 02108
(617) 727-3688

Michigan
525 W. Ottawa
Law Bldg.
Lansing, MI 48913
(517) 373-1110

Minnesota
102 State Capitol
St. Paul, MN 55155
(612) 297-4272

Mississippi
Gartin Bldg., 5th Fl.
Jackson, MS 39201
(610) 359-3680

Missouri
P.O. Box 899
Jefferson City, MO 65102
(314) 751-3221

Montana
215 N. Sanders St.
Helena, MT 59620
(406) 444-2026

Nebraska
Rm. 2115, State Capitol
Carson City, NV 68509
(702) 885-4170

Nevada
Capitol Complex P.O. Box 94906
Lincoln, NE 68509
(402) 471-2682

New Hampshire
208 State House Annex
235 Capitol St.
Concord, NH 03301
(603) 271-3658

New Jersey
Dept. of Law and Public
Safety
Justice Hughes Complex
CN080
Trenton, NJ 08625
(609) 292-4976

New Mexico
Bataan Memorial Bldg.
P.O. Box 1508
Santa Fe, NM 87501
(505) 827-6000

New York
Dept. of Law
State Capitol
Albany, NY 12224
(518) 474-7330

North Carolina
Dept. of Justice
2 E. Morgan St.
Raleigh, NC 27601
(919) 733-3377

North Dakota
1st Fl., State Capitol
600 E. Blvd.
Bismarck, ND 58505
(701) 224-2210

Ohio
30 E. Broad St., 17th Fl.
Columbus, OH 43266
(614) 466-3376

Oklahoma
112 State Capitol
Oklahoma City, OK 73105
(405) 521-3921

Oregon
Dept. of Justice
100 State Off. Bldg.
Salem, OR 97310
(503) 378-6002

Pennsylvania
Strawberry Sq., 16th Fl.
Harrisburg, PA 17120
(717) 787-3391

Rhode Island
72 Pine St.
Providence, RI 02903
(401) 274-4400

South Carolina
Dennis Bldg.
P.O. Box 11549
Columbia, SC 29211
(803) 734-3970

South Dakota
1st Fl., State Capitol
Pierre, SD 57501
(605) 773-3215

Tennessee
450 James Robertson Pkwy.
Nashville, TN 37219
(615) 741-6474

Texas
Box 12548, Capitol Station
Austin, TX 78711
(512) 463-2100

Utah
236 State Capitol
Salt Lake City, UT 84114
(801) 538-1324

Vermont
Pavilion Off. Bldg.
109 State St.
Montpelier, VT 05602
(802) 828-3171

Virginia
101 N. Eighth St. 5th Fl.
Richmond, VA 23219
(804) 786-2071

Washington
Hwy. Licenses Bldg.
M/S: PB-71
Olympia, WA 98504
(206) 753-2550

West Virginia
State Capitol Complex
Bldg. 1, Rm. E-26
Charleston, WV 25305
(304) 348-2021

Wisconsin
114 E. State Capitol
P.O. Box 7857
Madison, WI 53707
(608) 266-1221

Wyoming
State Capitol
Cheyenne, WY 82002
(307) 777-7810

APPENDIX B

CREDIT BUREAU ADDRESSES AND SAMPLE LETTERS

EQUIFAX CREDIT INFORMATION SERVICES
P.O. Box 740193
Atlanta, GA 30374-0193

For certified letters
5505 Peachtree Dunwoody
Suite 600
Atlanta, GA 30358
(404) 250-4000

TRANS UNION CREDIT
P.O. Box 8070
North Olmstead, OH 44070-8070

For certified letters
208 S. Market St.
Wichita, KS 67201

TRW CREDIT SERVICES
12606 Greenville Ave.
P.O. Box 749029
Dallas, TX 75374
(214) 235-1200

Most credits bureaus also have local offices. Consult your telephone book yellow pages under "Credit Bureaus." The charge varies from state to state. Call the bureau to find out how much to send.

Sample letters

A simple and concise letter is the best way to obtain a credit report quickly. Always give your name, current address, social security number, and previous address, if you haven't lived at your new address very long.

Requesting copy of credit report

Dear Sirs:

Please send me a copy of my most recent credit report. My social security number is xxx-xx-xxxx. My previous address is 1234 Oak Street, Anywhere, USA. Enclosed is $ [the fee in your state]. Thank you,

Sincerely,

Dispute letters

Dear Sirs:

I recently noticed that you are reporting an account on my credit report with American Express. I believe you have made an error, since this account does not belong to me. Please remove it from my credit file as soon as possible. Thank you.

Sincerely,

* * *

Dear Sirs:

You have an account listed with American Express on my credit report. I've never had an account with them. Perhaps I've been confused with someone else. Please take it off my credit file.

Sincerely,

Sound as natural as possible. Write in your own words and be brief and to the point.

APPENDIX C

CREDIT CARDS

5 lowest variable interest rate bank cards issued nationally (with a grace period)

Issuer	Rate	Annual Fee	Telephone
Simmons First National Pine Bluff, Ark.	10.5%v	$25	(501) 541-1304
Wachovia Card Services Newark, Del.	11.4%v	$39	(800) 842-3262
Bank of Hawaii Honolulu, Haw.	13.21%v	$45	(808) 543-9611
First National of Omaha, Nebraska	14.90%v	$20	(800) 688-7070
Valley Bank Las Vegas, NV	15.00%	$20	(702) 654-1165

5 lowest fixed interest rate bank cards issued nationally (with a grace period)

Issuer	Rate	Annual Fee	Telephone
People's Bank Bridgeport, CT	13.90%	$25	(800) 423-3273
National Bank of Alaska, Anchorage	14.50%	$20	(907) 276-1132
Ohio Savings Cleveland, Ohio	14.75%	$25	(800) 354-1445

First United Bank Bellevue, Neb.	14.88%	$20	(800) 635-8503
Wachovia Bank Salem, NC	14.88%	$25	(800) 241-7990

5 lowest rate gold cards issued nationally

Issuer	Rate	Annual Fee	Telephone
Central Carolina Bank Durham, NC	10.50%v	$20	(919) 683-7777
Simmons First National Pine Bluff, Ark.	10.50%v	$50	(501) 541-1304
Wachovia Card Services Newark, Del.	11.40%v	$49	(800) 842-3262
National Bank of Alaska	12.00%	$50	(907) 276-1132
Amalgamated Trust Chicago, IL	13.50%	$0	(800) 365-6464

5 lowest rate bank cards with no fee (with grace period)

Issuer	Rate	Annual Fee	Telephone
Amalgamated Trust Chicago, IL (Gold)	13.50%	$0	(800) 365-6464
USAA Federal Savings San Antonio, TX	13.70%v	$0	(800) 922-9092
Union Planters Nat. Memphis, Tenn.(Gold)	14.50%v	$0	(800) 628-8946
Fidelity National Atlanta, GA	17.90%	$0	(800) 753-2900
Security Bank & Trust Southgate, MI (Gold)	16.00%	$0	(800) 444-8060

Low cost, easier-to-get cards

Issuer	Rate	Annual Fee	Telephone
Wachovia Card Services Newark, Del.	11.40%v	$39	(800) 842-3262
USAA Federal Savings San Antonio, TX	13.70%	$0	(800) 922-9092
Citibank Sioux Falls, SD	19.80%	$20	(800) 321-2484

Secured credit cards nationally issued (with grace period)

Issuer	Interest	Annual Fee	Other Fees	Minimum. Deposit	Telephone
Continental Savings	16.00%	$0	$0	$1,000	(415) 239-4500
First Consumers	18.90%	$20	$0	$400	(800) 876-3262
American National	19.00%	$95	$0	$500	(914) 833-0560
First National Bank Marin	19.80%v	$25	$60	$300	(415) 459-6100
Bank of Hoven	21.00%	$35	$65	$380	(605) 948-2278
Home Trust S & L	21.00%	$35	$0	$400	(605) 692-9555
Farmers State Bank	21.80%	$35	$15	$350	(800) 544-1654
Key Federal Savings	21.99%	$35	$15	$500	(301) 939-4840
American Pacific Bank	18.9%	$30	$0	$400	(800) 879-8745
Community Bank Spirit Visa	14.9%	$49.95	$0	$500	(800) 779-8472
Consumer Fresh Start Ass.	18.9%	$30	$0	$400	(800) 352-5353
Dreyfus Thrift	19.8%	$25	$0	$500	(800) 727-3348

Selected secured credit card features and underwriting requirements

American National Bank

Program 1 — $500 minimum, 90 percent of deposit is credit line, $45 annual fee, 20-day grace period. Finance charges:

$500 to $1,250 deposit	prime plus 8 percent.
$1,251 to $2,500	prime plus 5 percent
$2,501 to $10,000	prime plus 3 percent
$10,000 to $25,000	prime plus 2 percent

Program 2 — $250 minimum, 100 percent of deposit is credit line, 19.8 percent interest, $69 annual fee, 20-day grace period.

Minimum underwriting requirements: No current judgments, liens, bankruptcies, chargeoffs of more than $250 in last 12 months.

American Pacific Bank

30-day grace period, rate is prime plus 8.5 percent.

Minimum underwriting requirements: Bankruptcy must be discharged, no serious recent delinquency, checking or savings account, verifiable street address, $1,000 minimum monthly income.

Community Bank

No late fees, overlimit fees or ATM fee.

Minimum underwriting requirements: No current delinquencies or unpaid income tax liens.

Consumer Fresh Start Association

Nonprofit association, money held in one-year CD, may be refunded in 18 to 24 months with good repayment history. No application fee but must join association ($40 per year). 30-day grace period.

Minimum underwriting requirements: Bankruptcy must be discharged.

Dreyfus Thrift

Cash advance fee of 2 percent, 25-day grace period.

Minimum underwriting requirements: No bankruptcy in the past six months.

Key Federal Savings

Savings account earns 4 percent up to $1,000, 5 percent over $1,000. 25-day grace period, no over limit fee.

Minimum underwriting requirements: Must earn $10,000 or more per year, bankruptcy discharged, no current delinquencies, no unpaid judgments or lients.

Bank of Hoven

Deposit earns 4.5 percent, late fee and over the limit fee $15, 25-day grace period.

Minimum underwriting requirements: Income of $7,500 a year or more.

BIBLIOGRAPHY

Allen, Micheal, "Bankruptcy Need Not be the Final Chapter on Credit", *The Wall Street Journal*, February 19, 1991, pp. C1

Berman, Daniel K., *The Credit Power Handbook*, 1989, CreditPower Publishing.

Berreby, David, "The Ordeal of the Credit Fraud Victim", *The New York Times*, September 4, 1988, pp.

Bruss, Robert J., "Overcoming Credit Hurdles in Buying a Home", *Los Angeles Times*, 1991 pp.

Canner, Glenn B. & Luckett, Charles A., "Consumer Debt Repayment Woes: Insights from a Household Survey", *Journal of Retail Banking*, Spring, 1990, pp. 55-63.

Caskey, John P., "Pawnbroking in America: The economics of a forgotten credit market", *Journal of Money, Credit & Banking*, February, 1991, pp. 85-99.

Chandler, Gary G. & Parker, Lee E., "Predictive Value of Credit Bureau Reports", *Journal of Retail Banking*, Winter, 1989, pp. 47-54.

"Consumers in the Information Age", *Credit Magazine*, November/December, 1990, pp. 26-28.

"Credit Reports: Getting it Half Right", *Consumer Reports*, July, 1991, pp. 453.

Crenshaw, Albert B., "Giving Credit Where Credit's Due", *The Washington Post*, June 17, 1990, pp. H11.

Crenshaw, Albert B., "More Banks Offer Secured Credit Cards", *The Washington Post*, February 18, 1990, pp. H15.

Cummings, Jack, *Complete Guide to Real Estate Financing*, 1978 Prentice Hall.

Daly, James, "The Brewing Battle for Better Data", *Credit Card Management*, January, 1991, pp. 46-52.

Davis, Kristin, "When the Credit Bureau Fouls Up", *Changing Times*, September, 1990, pp. 99-101.

Diamond, S.J., "Credit Bureaus' Tardy Rush to Aid Consumer", *Los Angeles Times*, October 11, 1991, pp. D1.

Diamond, S.J., "Debt Collectors Do Dirty Work for Creditors", *Los Angeles Times*, March 25, 1988, pp. D-1

Elias, Stephen, Albin, Renauer, & Leonard, Robin, *Bankruptcy*, 1989, Nolo Press.

Fanning, Deirdre, "Playing by the Rules", *Forbes*, March 9, 1987, pp. 76-78.

Fisk, Alan, "An Old Idea Revived: The Cashless Society.", *Canadian Banker*, October, 1986, Vol. 93 No. 5, pp. 30.

Fost, Dan, "Privacy Concerns Threaten Database Marketing", *American Demographics*, May, 1990, pp.18-21.

Garfinkel, Simson L., "Privacy Issue Caught in Credit Network", *Christian Science Monitor*, July 18, 1990, pp. 1.

Hartsfield, Jack, "New Breed of Inflation Fighters", *New Mexico Business Journal*, May, 1990, pp. 30.

Gould, Carol, "Going After That First Charge Card", *The New York Times*, October 30, 1988

Hansell, Saul, "Getting to Know You", *Institutional Investor*, June, 1991, pp. 71-86.

Hindo, Happy, "Loan Detectives Track Borrowers Who Skip Out", *Savings Institutions*, August 1986, pp. 80-83.

Hirsch, S., Equifax Company Report, Shearson Lehman Brothers, Inc., July 25, 1991.

"Keep Their Eyes Off Your Credit Data", *Money Magazine*, June, 1991.

Kurth, Walter, "Footprints in the Marketplace", *Credit*, May/June 1988, pp. 22-24.

Lauer, M., TRW Inc. Company Report, Kidder,Peabody & Company, Inc, July 25, 1991.

Lustgarten, E.S. TRW Inc. Company Report, Paine Webber Inc., July 31, 1991.

Maloney, Peter, "No Recession in Debt Collection", *United States Banker*, August, 1990, pp. 46-49.

McGrath, Anne, "Fixing Your Credit File", *U.S. News & World Report*, June 29, 1987, pp. 49

Miller, Micheal W., "Credit Report Firms Face Greater Pressure; Ask Norwich, Vt., Why.", *The Wall Street Journal*, September 23, 1991, pp. 1.

Miller, Micheal W., "Credit Reporting Industry Will Launch Campaign to Forestall New Regulations.", *The Wall Street Journal*, June 5, 1991, pB1 col. 3.

Miller, Micheal W., "IRS Appears to Break Rules on Credit Checks", *The Wall Street Journal*, May 7, 1991, pp. B1.

Mollard, Beth, "Here's a Laugh: All the Credit Cards are Paid Off", *Business First of Greater Columbus*, July 2, 1990, pp. 1.

Palmieri, Mario, "Lending Systems: Know the Score", *Banker's Monthly*, Febuary, 1991, pp. 30-31

Posch, Robert J., "Debt Collection Can be Stressful", *Direct Marketing*, June, 1990, pp. 65.

Prociv, S.J., "Three Generations: Evolution of the Credit Department", *Credit and Financial Management*, March, 1986, pp. 14-16.

Rodgers, Steve & Huehn, Kathryn, "Skip Tracing", *Credit Union Magazine*, Spetember, 1989, pp. 67-68.

Rosenblatt, Robert, "Better Consumer Guards in Credit Reports Urged", *The Los Angeles Times*, pp. D-1

Smith, Robert Ellis, "Consumer Credit Bureaus: Uncle Sam's 'Big Brother'", *Business and Society Review*, pp. 46-50.

Steinmetz, Thomas C., *The Mortgage Kit*, 1987, Longman Financial Services.

"The Cheapest Credit Cards", *Consumer's Research*, September, 1991, pp. 34.

The Credit Card Comparer, 1991, Consumer Credit Card Rating Service.

"TRW Sued on Ratings Unit", *The New York Times*, July 10, 1991.

Violano, Micheal, "The Best Bank Bounty Hunters", *Bankers Monthly*, August, 1990, pp. 57-59.

Warner, Ralph & Elias, Stephen, *Billpayer's Rights*, Nolo Press, 1986.

Williams, James R. & Bosold, Patrick E., "Faulty Files?", *Mortgage Banking*, August 1989, pp. 32-36

Yancey, Labat R., " Credit Clinics—The Challenge of Integrity", *Credit World*, May/June 1987, pp. 34-36.

ALSO AVAILABLE FROM ADAMS MEDIA

By Gordon K. Williamson

Low Risk Investing: How to get a good return on your money without losing any sleep.

In *Low Risk Investing*, Gordon Williamson clearly and concisely explains the many sound alternatives for achieving a good return on your money without any risk. He lays out the facts you need to evaluate scores of investment options. The author then rates each investment vehicle for security of principal, stability of income, total return, tax consequences, and as a hedge against inflation. Williamson also defines each investment in easy-to-follow language, explains how it works, clearly outlines its advantages and disadvantages, and details how the instrument is bought and sold. 5½" x 8½", 320 pages, paperback, $10.95.

The 100 Best Mutual Funds You Can Buy

Updated annually, *The 100 Best Mutual Funds You Can Buy* is the classic guide to selecting the very best funds. Gordon Williamson systematically reevaluates every one of the over 3,000 mutual funds on the market to determine an authoritative ranking of the top 100. Williamson then analyzes each of the 100 funds for total return, risk, quality of management, current income, and expense control. Find out just what funds are right for you. 6" x 9¼", 320 pages, paperback, $12.95.

Available wherever books are sold